Death of an Addict

Death of an Addict

Resurrection of a Man

Tio "Mr. CeaseFire" Hardiman

Violence Interrupters, NFP

Illinois

Death of an Addict, Resurrection of a Man
by Tio Hardiman
Published 2025 by Violence Interrupters, NFP
Chicago, Illinois 60617
http://violenceinterrupters.org

©2025 by Tio Hardiman

All rights reserved. No part of this book may be reproduced or transmitted in any form whatsoever without permission from the author except in the case of brief quotations embodied in articles, reviews, or books.

First Edition Published by Violence Interrupters, NFP

Printed in the United States of America

1 2 3 4 5 6 7 8 9 0

ISBN-13: 979-8-218-62031-8

Library of Congress Control Number: 20255907045

The information contained in this book has not been examined or approved by the Food and Drug Administration and is not intended to prevent, diagnose, or treat any medical condition or illness. Should you or a loved-one require medical advice or treatment, please seek the attention of a licensed medical professional.

To *my sister Tamar, my brother Tannan, and my uncle Leroy.*

Foreword

It's dangerous to tell people you can change if you want to. It takes more than a *want to*. I've worked extensively with people who are addicted to drugs – heroin, crack, cocaine, meth, the whole nine-yards! I've worked as a chaplain at the Cook County Jail, I've been criticized for starting an initiative to help prostitutes come off the streets, and much more. Change takes more than just want. It takes a spiritual move and foundation, a force greater than self. The people who tap into that greater power, the God power in their life, and use their will and determination achieve it.

    Throughout the years, I've watched person after person turn their lives around. I've also watched some of those who didn't, but I think there is no such thing as somebody cannot. There is no such thing as too far gone, too far out there. That's lies the enemy put on people. Anyone who draws the line and says, 'I want something better than this and I deserve better than this' can do it. It takes tapping into the God who called you to do better to bring you out. I am sure there are people who have done it without God, but the ones I know did it with their faith. Faith and Will together are what brings victory. Either we believe all things are possible through Christ or not. Many folks use drugs and alcohol which becomes their crutch and their god. They begin to serve cocaine, heroin, or a person; and that person runs and controls their life. That's their god.

I've witnessed numerous success stories. It is amazing how many people have been in what one would consider down and out situations (on the streets, lost everything, etc.) but they make that transformation and realize that what the scriptures promise is true. You can not only get back to where you were before addiction, but you can go even further.

Some years ago, we watched as the City of New Orleans was devastated by Hurricane Katrina. We saw horrific pictures of people stuck on the rooftops, trapped by the raging waters, pleading and begging to be rescued. Well, you can go out in the streets of Chicago – any city – and see all kinds of personal Katrinas that are wiping people out or seek to wipe them out. When I drive down to lower Wacker, the viaducts stand outside of the Pacific Gardens, which I have done, from 5:30 p.m. to 6:30 p.m. and watch the people walking in for bedding that night. Just around midnight, I drive and see those same horrific sights. There are people standing on the roofs of their own personal lives saying 'help'.

Some people may feel they don't deserve to come out of it because they've made so many poor choices and don't believe they deserve to have a better life. That is a lie from hell. God never changes what he wants for us. When you turn to God, you reminded that you don't have to compromise any of your hopes and dreams. God never changes His mind. There is a purpose and a destiny for us all, even addicts. God has placed them here with a purpose and the drug comes in to abort that purpose. You must ask yourself: "Do

I want to go back to my purpose, or do I want to have this perverted thing I've attached myself to? Do I want this to be what defines my life?"

For decades, I've gained national attention in the fight against violence and drugs; yet I marvel at God's miraculous intervention in Tio Hardiman's life. Tio is a living testament that change is possible. There are great talks and great sermons about transformation, how you can change your life and turn your life around; but the greatest sermon is being a life witness. Tio has spent time with folks who are in the same vulnerable situation he once was. It's one thing to change your life around and attempt to leave your background in the past, and another to stay with the folks on the street and in the communities who have been in similar situations to be a living witness that they can change as you have. I have an appreciation that Tio is not only saying that it can be done, but he is someone living it and helping others. His discipline and determination are what enabled him to transform. I don't know if he is faith-wise, but what I do see in Tio is a person of great passion and conviction. Whether he acknowledges it or not, I see his Christ-like care for others. I've seen this in him time and time again. He's really got that compassion and heart of Christ for people, along with tremendous experience. I believe these are his real gift – his compassion and Christ-like heart for people.

I was once told that Tio has been running all his life. When people are running, they are running from ever having to come face-to-face with loving themselves. You don't have to run anymore. Let God continue to use you and realize that God has a very, very special purpose for you. Achieve the purpose for which God called you into this life and don't settle for less. There's an 'A' plan for our lives; why settle for a 'Z' plan?

Father Michael L. Pfleger
Saint Sabina Church, 1210 W. 78th Place

Contents

Preface i

Introduction 1

Part I: Birth of an Addict 3

   Cabrini Green Rowhouses 5

   Lon City 11

   Father Figures 23

   My Biggest Regret 31

   The Glam Drug 39

Part II: Life of an Addict 47

   Magic Carpet 49

   Black Gold 53

   Rock Bottom 57

Part III: Death of an Addict 67

   Giving Up Addiction 69

   The Aftermath 81

      Tracing My Roots 93

   Facing My Trauma 105

   Giving Back 111

   The Great Fall 119

   Hardiman for Governor 127

Message to People Suffering from Drug Addiction 137

Acknowledgements 141

About the Author 143

References 145

Preface

Drug addiction is a disease that is characterized by the uncontrollable impulse to use a substance despite its negative impacts. And when you resort to drug use to cope with life's rollercoaster, the chances that addiction will come along for the ride becomes more substantial. And once you become addicted, you'll begin to morph into someone outside of your natural self and become unrecognizable. Then no matter how much you'll want to change back to your sober self, choosing sobriety over your drug of choice will become ten times more difficult. This is because it's not enough to simply want to change. Sobriety takes a lot of effort, patience, and will. It's something you must fight for each day, and none of us truly knows how much fight we have within us until we're fighting for our lives.

This book is explicit in nature; parental guidance is suggested. The content is in no way meant to glorify or endorse illicit drug use. It includes the compelling details of Tio Hardiman's personal journey of survival through drug addiction and trauma. It is broken into three parts: *Birth of an Addict* in which he shares the precursors from his early years that made him vulnerable to drug use; *Life of an Addict* in which he describes how he spiraled into a life of drug addiction; and *Death of an Addict* in which he shares how he overcame addiction to become the man he is today.

If you or a loved-one is suffering from addiction, there are many free, confidential services available to assist you. Call SAMHSA's National Helpline (1-800-662-4357). They will connect you to mental health and/or drug treatment centers and programs in your local area.

Introduction

We are all constantly under the influence of something. Before you left your mother's womb, you were under the influence of how she cared for herself and you as her unborn child. Chances are, if she was in a thriving and loving environment, was well-rested and nourished, was thrilled about becoming a parent, and was surrounded by love and support, the energy of these influences were transferred to you prior to birth; and that loving, supportive environment and energy would translate into an opportunity for you to also thrive. If she was impoverished, malnourished, and her life was full of stress and turmoil, chances are you were also highly impacted.

Once we all press through the canal of life and enter this world, we are exposed to another set of influences. Some of the most prevalent influences we are exposed to are the influences we connect with in our environments and atmosphere, the influences of societal expectations and stereotypes, and, most importantly, the influences of the family we were born into. I was born into a set of circumstances that exposed me to drugs and violence at a very young age. Majority of the influential figures in my life, including my family members, suffered from drug and alcohol addiction. Some of them died from it.

Despite the adverse influences drug addiction has on health, familial relationships, safety, careers, etc., 21 million Americans have at least one addiction. More than 70 percent of people who've tried an illicit drug before the age of 13 have an addiction to alcohol and/or drugs. Thousands of people die every year from drug overdose and millions more are affected by drug addiction in some way. Out of the millions of Americans who suffer from addiction, only 10% receive treatment. In fact, alcohol, the most widely used substance, is the most common addiction left untreated.

In the U.S. alone, more than 3 million deaths annually can be attributed to substance use. Opioid drugs, both illegal and prescribed, account for 24% of all addictions. Over the past two decades, there has been an uptick in opioid overdoses, causing the Department of Health and Human Services to declare opioid addiction a health crisis. Out of the 10 million people who misuse opioids each year, 50,000 die from them. Sixty-eight percent of those deaths were caused by synthetic opioids, as an estimated 902,000 people in the United States use heroin on a regular basis resulting in 15,000 deaths each year. In 2021, 1.4 million people reported having a cocaine use disorder. The same year, 24,486 people died of cocaine overdose.

Years ago, my life also hung in the balance of my addiction. I could've been another death statistic, but I was spared.

Part I: Birth of an Addict

Cabrini Green Rowhouses

I was born on September 21, 1962 to my birthmother, Carolyn Burch. Chicago was my birthplace, and it is still my home to this day. From birth until I was 5 years old, my siblings and I lived in the Cabrini Green Rowhouses on N Mohawk Avenue with our mother who was raised in the South by both her parents prior to moving to Chicago. This had a tremendous impact on her mindset and worldview.

She was an attractive woman: short in stature, chocolate skin tone, straight, black hair, and brown, almond shaped eyes. It seemed that men found her irresistible. She was drawn to the type of men who lived the fast life – drug dealers, gamblers, drug addicts, etc. You know, the kind of men who drove Cadillac Fleetwoods. She was

Part I: Birth of an Addict

also a fanatic of American actors and sports legends, Jim Brown and Fred Willamson. She loved them so much that I also began to admire them.

During the late 60's, Cabrini Green was a majority African American housing project surrounded by predominately Caucasian, affluent communities. It was notorious for drugs and criminal activity. I passed the time observing the hustle and bustle of the city beneath my bedroom window. I observed endless lines of people standing outside of drug houses waiting their turns to purchase illegal drugs, including heroin which was the drug of choice for many. I witnessed many street fights right in front of our home. The deafening noise from fire trucks, ambulances, and other city emergency vehicles was constant. The cool guys drove by in their Cadillacs. Oblivious to their lifestyles, I thought they were all wealthy businessmen. I can recall staring at the skyscrapers in downtown Chicago and dreaming of visiting that area one day. My mother vowed that she would take me there.

To my knowledge, my mother never used drugs, but she was also hardly ever home. She was always working, I suppose. When I asked her what she did for a living, she told me that she was a beautician. As I got older, I noticed that she spent a chunk of her time with ladies of the night.

My siblings and I spent most of our time at home alone with no adult supervision. None of us were over the age of 8. There were seven of us at the time: my brother Tee was the oldest followed by my brother Tannan, my sister Tamar, my sister Tarita, then me, my sister Ladrena, my brother John, my brother Richard, my sister Karla, my sister Monica, and the youngest was my brother Jeffrey. However, Tee and Tannan never lived with the rest of us. They were raised by my aunt Evelyn from very young ages, which made my sister Tamar the oldest sibling in the household.

We lived in squalor. Our rowhouse was completely ransacked and infested with cockroaches, rats, and other pests. The stench of dirty diapers, mounds of trash, soiled clothing, and dirty dishes was ever present, as these items could be found lying about.

Food was scarce and my siblings and I were severely malnourished. We older children survived on grilled cheese sandwiches made of thick government cheese, rice & beans, restaurant food, and luncheon meat whenever these items were available, while my younger siblings were still drinking from infant bottles. The rats ate anything that was left on the table.

We did not receive routine medical care. At times, we suffered through symptoms of a common cold for months. I can hardly remember a time when all our noses weren't dripping with mucus. My sister Tarita had a persistent cough that never seemed to go away.

Because we received government assistance, no men were allowed to live in the home and the social services agency sent

Part I: Birth of an Addict

inspectors to ensure strict adherence to this guideline. One day, a slender Caucasian woman with short, brunet hair dressed in a black, knee-length skirt and baby blue, collared blouse came to the house. My mother warned us to sit quietly on the living room sofa as the social worker went from room to room, searching closets and looking under beds for signs of a man's presence. Once she did not find anything and the coast was clear, we all went back to our regularly scheduled program.

My siblings and I played most of the day, jumping on beds, hiding under tables, and anything else we could think of to pass time while our mother was away. This pattern continued until one day, our grandparents showed up and took control. They drove to our mother's house, gathered all us children and our belongings, placed everything in the bed of my grandfather's pickup truck, and hauled us away to Chicago's south side. They removed us from our mother's care and took us into their home for the remainder of childhood.

In the United States, neglect is the most prevalent form of child abuse and is more than four times likely to be reported than any other type of child abuse including physical, sexual, and psychological maltreatment. It causes severe damage within children but receives the least amount of attention in policy and practice. Child neglect causes physical and psychological impairments, impacts executive functioning and self-regulation skills, and disrupts the body's stress response. It also causes dysfunction in emotional and interpersonal skills. Yet, children who have experienced neglect often go untreated.

My siblings and I were unaware that our mother's consistent absence and our deplorable living conditions were considered child neglect; they were our norm. This was our way of life. But we were more than happy to move in with our grandparents. Happy to have food, safety, structure, and adults who cared enough to show up.

What we didn't understand then was that the neglect we lived through had already rewired our bodies and minds. As children, we had no language for trauma. We didn't know that constant hunger, fear, and unpredictability created a biological storm inside a child. Science later gave it a name: toxic stress.

When a child endures long periods of chaos, lack of safety, or emotional abandonment, the body floods with cortisol, the hormone designed to help us survive danger. Cortisol is useful in short bursts; but when neglect forces a child's body to release it day after day, year after year, it becomes damaging.

We were living in filth, caring for ourselves, jumping at every sound in the hallway, and never knew when our mother would return, so our bodies adapted to survive. Our cortisol levels stayed high because our brains believed the danger never ended. This kind of prolonged stress changes the architecture of children's brains. It weakens memory, delays development, and makes it more difficult to regulate emotions and foster trust with other people. It teaches the

Part I: Birth of an Addict

body to stay alert, even long after the threat is gone. That is what child neglect does. Trains a child to survive, not to thrive.

By the time our grandparents rescued us, the damage had already woven itself into our nervous systems. We were safe but also felt overwhelmed. We were sensitive to noise, constantly hungry, and deeply unsure of ourselves. We didn't understand routine or affection. We didn't understand why adults suddenly cared whether we bathed, brushed our teeth, or ate three meals a day. We were children learning basic skills that most kids take for granted.

Yet, children are resilient; we were not an exception. In our grandparents' home, the cortisol inside our bodies finally had a chance to settle and the constant alarms inside our heads quieted, little by little. The structure and care they gave us didn't just feed us—it healed us. It began to undo the silent damage that had been done in the darkness of neglect.

Healing, however, is never instant. The effects of childhood neglect follow you into adulthood: into relationships, into self-worth, into the way you respond to stress. It shapes how you move through the world, and how the world moves through you. But understanding what happened—naming it, calling it what it was—gives power back to the survivor.

Lon City

My maternal grandparents, Harry & Gladyes Burch, were originally from Georgia. My grandfather was from Covington and my grandmother, Atlanta. The two met at a party when my grandfather came home from the U.S. Army. During the 1940s, they wed and migrated to Chicago to find work. They lived on Chicago's south side and were well-known throughout the community. They were a perfect match.

My grandfather was a tall man with a dark complexion who prided himself on being physically strong. He was a hard-working businessman. He wasn't a very affectionate man but was a great provider for our family. He was always proud of himself and often boasted of being his own man, not working for anyone else. Instead, he sold fresh vegetables, fish, and refurbished appliances. "Fresh fish jumped out the water and I caught it", he'd announce to potential customers as he drove through their neighborhoods with a pickup truck full of goods. He employed many family members, including my uncles and cousins, whenever there was a need.

The result of an unforgettable encounter with my grandfather taught me to ask for exactly what I wanted. I was about eight years old and had asked him for five dollars. I displayed a look of disappointment when he pulled out a wad of money and gave me exactly five dollars. "Is that all you can give?" I asked. Once he observed my expression and pondered my words, he slapped me

Part I: Birth of an Addict

upside the head and said, "I gave you what you asked for! If you wanted more, you should've asked for more."

My grandmother was a remarkable woman and one of my greatest mentors. She truly believed in the importance of family. Her maiden name prior to marrying my grandfather was Goodwill and her brother, Charles Goodwill, once lived in the basement of our home. Another family member, Aunt Willabell, who was in her senior years, once stayed in one of the bedrooms towards the back of the house.

My grandmother was a nurturer. She was the main caretaker in the household; she made sure everyone had a hot meal prepared for dinner. There were so many people living there that sometimes I'd be left with the chicken's gizzards, neck, or livers but it didn't matter; I was happy to have a plate. She was an amazing cook, and I was grateful to be provided with a hot, wholesome meal. How she was able to manage our household while working as an employee of the Dial Soap Company, I'll never know.

My siblings and I adjusted well to our grandparents' home for the most part. We all played together but my sister Tarita and I were the closest. She was only one year older than me. We were 6 and 7 years old when our grandparents came to save us. We had only been living there for one week when a major tragedy struck.

Lon City

"Ready or not; here I come!" Tarita and I played hide and seek, and it was my turn to seek. I searched for her in the bedroom; she wasn't there. I ran to the bathroom and the door was locked, but the sound of Uncle Leroy's angelic voice seeping through the cracks of the door let me know she was not the person inside. I ran into the kitchen and could hear a faint giggle coming from under the table. "Found you!" Tarita scrambled and giggled; then suddenly went silent. She lay on the floor pretending to be asleep.

"Tarita ... get up." I shook her but she just continued laying there. I tried again ... "Tarita! Stop playing! Get up!" Her body was limp, mouth slightly ajar and eyes rolled up into her head. I tried again but she didn't move. "Grandma! ... Something's wrong with Tarita!"

I called out to my grandmother once I realized Tarita was not joking. My grandmother was in the front room at the time and hurried to the kitchen. Once she assessed the situation, she called the paramedics. The paramedics arrived and began resuscitation efforts. I watched from the front room while my grandparents and uncles created a semi-circle around Tarita's body in the kitchen.

"Clear! One, one thousand, two one thousand, three one thousand." They attempted breathing apparatuses and mechanical chest compressions. Nothing. Tarita was pronounced dead on the scene.

My eyes swelled with tears. I glanced in and took one last look at my sister as she lay there with her eyes wide open. It was

Part I: Birth of an Addict

later found that the cause of death was the untreated cough that never seemed to go away. It was pneumonia.

A few weeks later, our family and members of the community crowded Dotty Nash Funeral Home to say our goodbyes. My siblings and I sat in the front row with our mother and grandparents. In front of us sat a child-sized, brown, wooden casket. Inside was my sister Tarita adorned in a beautiful white dress accessorized with pink tights and black shoes and her black hair neatly combed back away from her face. She resembled a fairytale princess but was resting peacefully.

I was too young to understand the impact of losing my sister. I did not know what to think, say, or do. I recall that there were sorrowful moments during the homegoing, but not a lot. Mom broke down in spurts. My grandparents offered gestures of comfort and tried to remain strong for us all.

Although I'm sure that it was an emotional time for our family, I do not recall any prolonged, deep feelings or expressions of sadness. I simply recall my mother saying, "You won't see Tarita anymore. She's gone with God now."

As time went on, my family seemed to heal from this tragedy, or at least we spoke about it less and less. My remaining siblings and I continued living with our grandparents and my playmates became Tamar and John.

Lon City

Since education was very important to my grandmother, she enrolled us all into private school at St. Felicitas Catholic School. We may not have been the top scholars there and we wore the same dingy uniforms each day, but we all did well. And with our grandparents' guidance, Tamar seemed to adjust well and no longer had to supervise her younger siblings. She was practically a baby herself.

My mother continued to have children. After a few years, my younger siblings Ladrena, Ricky, and John came to live with us and our grandparents also. Later, my mother gave birth to Karla, Monica, and Jeffrey, but she raised them herself.

I didn't realize that my brothers Tee and Tannan didn't live with us and were permanently living with our Aunt Evelyn until I was 11 years old. Aunt Evelyn would bring the two to visit. I never forged a strong relationship with either of my older brothers; they just weren't around that often and there was a significant age gap between us.

Part I: Birth of an Addict

My grandparents' sons, Michael, Bobby, Billy, and Leroy lived in the home as well. Their oldest son, Harry Jr., was the only one who did not live there. He was enlisted in the army. When we first moved in, my uncles Bobby, Billy, and Leroy worked for my grandfather for a living, while my uncle Michael attended high school. Their presence made the home busy and lively, but it was harmless fun. At least that's what appeared on the surface. I later discovered that they were addicts.

My first time witnessing my uncle Leroy shooting heroin, I was about 8 years old. I stared through the bathroom door as he tied a rubber tube around his arm until a big vein appeared, used a needle to extract fluid from a bottle cap, and injected it into his arm. He began to relax, and his head began to nod as he entered a trance-like state. I heard him say, "Oh, baby. This is good." More and more, this became a common occurrence with my uncles. I used to think they were asleep while standing.

My uncle Michael, however, was the only uncle who was not addicted to substances at the time of our arrival. He was a tall, chubby guy with a dark complexion. He was my grandparents' youngest son and ten years older than me. He was a star football athlete and an amazing guitar player who graduated with honors. He was considered the golden child. That is, until my siblings and I showed up disrupting his life. There were obvious signals that he had become jealous that my siblings and I commanded so much of our grandparents' attention; he began to target me.

One day I entered the kitchen where Michael and his friends were congregating. Michael grabbed two slices of bread and a container of Morton's salt from the cupboard. He dumped a large amount of salt onto one of the slices, placed the other slice atop, and made me eat every morsel right there in front of his friends, no water to chase it down. This became a common occurrence.

If he wasn't terrorizing me with salt sandwiches, he would give me an old-fashioned beat down. In my preteen years, my friends Roy, Philip and I used to steal expensive merchandise off freight trains and Michael would use a large speaker to deter us, impersonating a police officer. Once we dropped the merchandise and ran, he would retrieve it and sell it for himself.

I loathed Michael. He was a bully and a coward. I told my mother about the salt sandwiches, but she did nothing to protect me. So, once I entered my early teen years and gained some strength, I began to fight back.

One day, Michael's best friend Chip and I were shooting dice, and I won. I was around 14 years old at the time. Chip became angry and began tussling with me. He snatched my money, and the tussling turned to real blows. Michael came out of the house and witnessed what was happening but did nothing to help me. I became so angry that he didn't help defend me that I picked up a 2x4 and

Part I: Birth of an Addict

attempted to bash Michael's head in. I had reached my breaking point.

I hadn't done anything to Michael; my mere existence was enough for him to want to punish me. We were supposed to be family, yet he was allowing one of his friends to attack me for winning a bet fair and square. When I picked up that 2x4 and swung at his skull, the force behind it wasn't just the frustration that had built up in that moment, but the years of hurt I endured suffering at his hands. Once the tool connected with his head, I didn't stick around to see him drop; I ran off in fear for my life. I later snuck back into the house through the back door but there were no repercussions. Michael was never the same after that.

Throughout the years, I learned a lot from my uncles. Notably, Uncle Leroy taught me how to hustle and make money without selling drugs. But my uncles were constantly undermining and stealing from one another, which led to many petty disputes. They occupied the basement most nights because Uncle Billy and Uncle Leroy slept there. Each night they gambled and drank alcohol with other slippery characters.

Uncle Billy didn't work and didn't socialize with us much. He resold furniture for my grandfather's business to earn a living and support his drug problem. He would spend the longest time in the bathroom shooting dope and who knows what else? He kept a stash of dirty magazines.

Lon City

Uncle Bobby was a Vietnam War veteran who had received an honorable discharge from the U.S. Army. He initially worked at the post office when he returned home but soon became addicted to heroin too. Thereafter, he lost his job and began burglarizing homes to support his habit. He was a good uncle to us. He sometimes bathed us before we went to school, and when he witnessed them, he defended me against Michael's attacks. "We not doing that today!" He would warn Michael.

You could always tell when he was high. He would sing Marvin Gaye songs and other soul music to the top of his lungs. I believe he dreamed of becoming one of The Temptations.

Uncle Bobby once robbed a group of painters. Because he had accumulated paint all over shoes and clothes, the police were able to trace his tracks from the crime scene to the dope house, and then to our house. "Where is Robert Burch? We know he's here because we see the paint tracks!" The officers insisted. When they took him into custody, I grabbed the money he had stolen and kept it for myself.

I gravitated toward Uncle Leroy; I considered him the cool uncle. He had spent some time in the penitentiary not long after we began living with our grandparents but returned when I was about 14 years old. I was present for his homecoming. He was dressed flamboyantly in a brown and white disco shirt and was already a heroin addict. However, even in addiction, he always had money.

Part I: Birth of an Addict

He earned a living and supported his drug habit by becoming a loan shark – lending money to people and tacking on a ridiculous amount of interest. He was also my grandfather's go-to for the grocery business. When I spent time with him, we often visited his girlfriend Alice's house who lived only a few blocks away. Once my grandfather died in my later teen years, Uncle Leroy took over the family business and became known as Fish Man. During brutally cold Chicago winters, he would start a fire in a garbage can behind the alley and still sell fish, fruit and vegetables. Customers thought that he had caught the fish, but I know that he really got it from the market on 39th Street.

My grandparents accepted my uncles as they were. They never judged them or threatened to evict them. By the age of 12, I was strong enough to pull the strap tight, and my uncles depended on me to help them produce a good vein to shoot their dope, or they'd ask that I hold one of their arms nice and steady as they injected themselves. I couldn't help but think that Tarita was spared the exposure to drug addiction; she would've grown up around it, too.

My mother remained in our lives on a sporadic basis. At times, she would retrieve my siblings and I from our grandparents' house to catch a movie or to eat at Ronnie's Steak House. She didn't spend a lot of time with us, and I often longed to see her. There were many Christmas holidays that she vowed that she would come. I would be left disappointed looking out the window waiting for her. As

Lon City

we continued living with our grandparents, she continued with her life, dating known street criminals.

Father Figures

Every boy needs his father. In his book, "Life without Father", David Popenoe highlights evidence that suggests that children benefit when both of their biological parents live in the household, and the damaging impacts when fathers are not present. Boys particularly benefit when their biological fathers are present and involved. They tend to be exposed to more positive life experiences and benefits than those who do not live with their fathers. Some of these benefits include college graduation, less idleness, and less involvement in the criminal justice system. Contrarily, boys whose biological fathers are not present or involved are more susceptible to less college, less work, and more prison.

When I was about 8 years old, John, Tamar, and I began to spend our summers with our mother in Cabrini Green Rowhouses. At that time, our mother was married to a man named Freddie, also known as, Frantic Freddie. Freddie also had a son of his own, Lutuh Shaw, who was a bit older than I. He was raised alongside my siblings and me, but I never really spent much time with him due to our age difference.

Other than our grandfather, our stepfather was the closest we had to an example of a father figure. He was 6'2, a tall man with a brown complexion who weighed about 230 pounds. He and Mom had met the previous year and wed shortly thereafter. He lived up to the moniker, "Frantic". He was addicted to heroin and had a reputation

Part I: Birth of an Addict

for being extremely impulsive or quick to act without thinking things through first. People were afraid of him; he didn't hesitate to use violence against anyone who offended him or his family. Freddie was a functioning heroin addict. He hustled for a living, earning enough money to support his family and fuel his addiction.

My grandfather and Freddie were good providers; yet I yearned for a relationship with my biological father although I never really knew him. My mother had lived a promiscuous lifestyle and was honest that she wasn't sure who my actual biological father was. When I was about 9 years old, she disclosed to me that she believed my father was one of two men: John Stewart or Robert Hardiman.

Robert Hardiman, aka Hawk, was a well-known tough guy and lady's man who ran the streets of Chicago. He could usually be found hanging out somewhere near 39th & Langley. He had a light complexion and was of a medium build. He was muscular and kept his mustache well-groomed. He made lamps and was a good photographer and artist. Although we did not have a deep connection, every now and again he would take me with him and show me how to fix lamps and take photographs.

My mother was clear that Hawk was my older sister Tamar's father, but uncertain if he was mine. Despite this, he appeared to own the naming rights of us all. He is the reason most of us have a name that begins with the letter T. However, as a young boy, I was quickly reminded that Hawk would never provide me with the loving influence and support I needed from my father. He didn't have the selflessness or capacity required to do so.

When I was about 8 years old, he reached out to our mother and requested to come get Tamar and me so we could spend time with him and our paternal grandparents, aunts, and uncles, etc. He arrived to pick us up during the late morning and had purchased a box of donuts for us to consume for breakfast. We were thrilled to not only be with our dad, but that we were going to meet the rest of our family.

Once we arrived, Hawk left us there without any explanation. A lady named Bernice, a woman I believe was his sister, snatched our donuts and called us "ugly, light-skinned mutha fuckers" to our faces. She said she was going to see what we were made of. I didn't know what that meant, but I knew it didn't sound pleasant. She made it clear that she did not like us. But she didn't even know us; how could she treat children who were supposed to be a part of her family this way?

The kitchen was a small area with beige countertops, unkept beige floors, and green cabinets. A tiny, white stove sat near the sink and a yellow refrigerator sat near the entrance. Space heaters sat near the windows which were adorned with thick, dark curtains. A small, round table and matching chairs with metal legs and cushions covered in vinyl sat near the walls which were covered in wallpaper.

Part I: Birth of an Addict

Bernice grabbed two kitchen chairs and positioned them with the backs touching each other. She forced Tamar to sit in one and I in the other. To ensure we wouldn't try to leave or run for help, she grabbed some extension cord and a belt. She weaved the chord and belt in and out of the seats and backs of the chairs, wrapped it around our arms, and tied it tight. She left us and never returned.

The space heaters were doing their job, roasting us. Tamar and I sat there in the unbearable heat, tied up and unable to move, sweating profusely for hours. Alone and afraid, we wondered what would happen next. We didn't know how to escape; the chords were just too tight. *Where is Hawk?* I thought.

The worst part of us being held captive in this situation wasn't necessarily the mental, verbal, and now physical abuse. It was that no one in that household seemed to care. No one came to check on us. No one came into the kitchen and offered us anything to eat or drink. No one asked how we were doing. No one came to free us or to tell us it was a bad joke. It was almost as if we weren't there at all. Why would Hawk bring us here in the first place if his intention wasn't to spend time with us?

Hours later, as we sat still tied to the chairs trying to think of a master plan of escape, a fire erupted! The blaze which appeared to start near the curtains quickly spread, consuming a nearby couch and everything in its path. Within minutes the entire house was filled with thick, black smoke and we couldn't breathe. "Help!" We yelled and cried, but no one came for us. We had been left there to die.

As we coughed and gagged from the fumes, a hand reached in and grabbed us both. Firefighters and paramedics pulled us before the smoke and flames overtook us, saving our lives. They rushed us to the hospital where we were treated for smoke inhalation. Mom and my stepfather, Freddie, were contacted and they met us there at the hospital. Hawk was nowhere to be found.

John Stewart was my other potential biological father. He was known on the streets by the name, Beetsy. I resembled him in a sense; he also had a light complexion. He was a heroin addict with a criminal background who did not come around often, maybe twice a year at best. Because he knew there was a great possibility that he was my biological father, he took me around his family, and they accepted me as one of their own.

A memory that I recall with John is when I was about 8 years old and he took me to Burger King. It was my first time trying a Whopper; I've been in love with them ever since. Afterwards, he took me to a dope house. I sat outside on the stoop while he went inside to get high. During different periods of his life, John attempted sobriety but relapsed each time. He died from a heart attack while riding public transportation. He was only a little over 50 years old.

Part I: Birth of an Addict

One of John's cousins, Irving Napue, aka Scadoolee, was a key player in the drug game back then. He was what we referred to as a *made man*, a well-respected leader. His notoriety came from the no-nonsense approach he took to keep his soldiers in line. An avid jogger and swimmer, he was also  known for being physically fit. He preferred wearing silver jewelry instead of gold. I admired Scadoolee; he called me his little cousin.

Freddie remained a constant father figure and provider during our summers with Mom on the mid-western side of Chicago. Despite his addiction, he remained aware of what was happening in the household and vowed to protect us at all costs. He stayed informed of the most current events in the neighborhood as well. Although we were not his biological children, he treated us as his own.

During the summer of fifth grade, while in the care of my mother and Freddie, Mom sent me to the neighborhood corner store to purchase a few items. On my way there, I was assaulted by a stranger twice my age and size who beat me up and stole the money Mom had given me to purchase groceries.

When Freddie got home and saw that I had a black eye, he was livid. He demanded to know immediately who had assaulted me. Before Mom could finish telling him the story, he grabbed me by the arm, dragged me to his Cadillac Fleetwood, and began combing the streets for the assailant.

An informant told him where to find the culprit, who was seated in the back of a local pool hall and in a semi-conscious dope feign nod. Freddie asked me to identify the man as the one who had attacked me. I said, "Yes, that's the muthafucker!" I then stood by and watched Freddie unload bullets into the guy's torso, killing him in cold blood. We immediately fled the scene, got back into the car and drove back home as if nothing had happened. That night, Freddie was arrested. He was later found guilty of first-degree murder and sentenced to prison.

Desensitization occurs when we have reduced emotional or physical responses to an event after being exposed to it frequently, causing us to become less sensitive to the pain and suffering of others. I had been exposed to so much violence that I had become desensitized. I had no remorse for the man who had attacked me. I carried the sentiment "shit happens" with me later, throughout much of my adulthood.

A few years after Freddie's imprisonment, my mother met and wed a man named George Dandridge. George became the pillar of our family and was the biological father of my younger brother. He was mild mannered and always wore white shoes and checkered pants. I recall that in 1979, he purchased my first leather jacket. It

Part I: Birth of an Addict

was light blue fake leather, or what we called pleather, but I looked stylish in it.

George was a gambler who bet on horses. He usually returned from the racetrack with wads of money from his winnings. Once he introduced my mom to his vice, she started going every day, hoping some of George's luck would transfer to her. Mom and George were inseparable but for some odd reason, they argued every single day of their marriage. They, however, stayed together for 25 years until George's death.

My Biggest Regret

My older sister Tamar and I were three years apart and inseparable. When I was around 7 years old, we loved to play in the backyard and shared hopes and dreams of how we'd like to live our lives in the future. We'd also curl up on our grandmother's couch together and watch scary shows and movies. Some of our memorable favorites were Creature Feature, Count Dracula, and Frankenstein. We also watched our favorite television shows. Our absolute favorite was *The Little Rascals*. Whenever we were going to watch it, Tamar would pop popcorn. Her favorite characters were Alfalfa and Buckwheat, and mine was Spanky. We watched cartoons such as *Bugs Bunny* and *The Jetsons*, too.

Tamar and I had forged a very strong bond. She was very protective of me and although I was younger, I was protective of her too. She was a beautiful girl, inside and out. She was a kind, quiet

Part I: Birth of an Addict

soul with outward beauty in the likeness of Jada Pinkett-Smith – short in stature, light complexion, and dark, curly hair.

When I was about 12 years old, our lives took a drastic turn. Suddenly, my grandmother fell terminally ill and could no longer do the things she enjoyed such as planting flowers and vegetables in our garden and heading all major family functions and holiday gatherings as the proud matriarch. She was the one who washed our clothes, ensured we ate breakfast, and saw us off to school each morning. She was the one who woke us up on Sunday mornings to attend Catholic church. But around this time, the rock of our family had stopped coming out of her bedroom. From time to time, I would knock on the door to check on her and she'd always respond, "I'll be out in a minute."

Nurses visited and assisted with her care, but she was dying of stomach cancer and there was nothing that anyone could do to ease her pain. I believe she had decided to die at home.

One day, my grandmother came out of her bedroom and fell to the floor. I was there to pick her up and noticed that she had left a trail of blood. I did my best to assist her with bathing, but she was fragile. She had a medium build when she was healthy, but the cancer had eaten away at her; she appeared to be skin and bones.

My grandmother's terminal illness was the catalyst of a spiraling household. The warmth and security she brought to our lives had become cold and unfathomable. Our home, which was

My Biggest Regret

once full of vitality, had become a quiet, desolate place and our family began to unravel.

My grandfather's alcoholism became more apparent and destructive. I don't think he realized the effects that his drinking had on the household, including us as the children who bear witness to it. He gambled a lot and got into arguments. I even witnessed him slice a few men in the gut, including a man we called Chucky Bell who tried to steal from him. The alcohol blinded him to the fact that our basement was becoming a place for drug addicts to hang out – much like a trap house. My grandfather began spending time in the basement with them, too.

I began experimenting with marijuana and alcohol, my uncles continued their heavy drug use, and Michael began using cocaine. Tamar was becoming far from the sweet sister I once knew. Before she even hit her teenage years, I noticed my uncles' friends eyeballing her, lusting after her. Although I was younger than her, I tried to protect her by confronting them.

When Tamar was about 14 years old, the boldest of the dope feigns began meeting with her in her bedroom, behind closed doors. He had been grooming her: talking to her as if she was an adult, making her feel special and heard, as if he didn't have an agenda of his own. With Uncle Bobby's backing, I'd break up these meetings. I kicked her bedroom door open and would warn them to "get the fuck out".

Part I: Birth of an Addict

My uncle Bobby unexpectedly met his death before my grandmother when one of his burglary attempts went left. He attempted to burglarize the home of an armed man and was shot twice in the back of the head as he tried to escape. He died on the scene.

Uncle Bobby's death was an additional dark cloud over our family and household, and I was tasked with sharing the tragic news with my grandmother. Most parents deny favoring one child over another, but I believe that Bobby was my grandmother's favorite. And when I broke the news of his death, she was at a loss for words and stopped breathing. She gasped for air then she belted out a heart-wrenching scream. She died a few short weeks later.

Once my grandmother died, our home became dope feign central, addicts began hanging out there day and night. Since Bobby was no longer with us, there was little I could do to protect Tamar. The addicts eventually got to her and took advantage of her sexually. She turned to heroin and became an addict too.

I first noticed Tamar had become an addict when I witnessed her at the tender age of 16 standing against a wall in the basement with blood pouring from her veins as I watched her nod back and forth in a trance. She began dressing more provocatively – wigs, miniskirts, makeup, etc. – for what I refer to as the hoe stroll. All types of men began picking her up in Cadillacs and she wouldn't return home for days at a time.

My Biggest Regret

When our grandmother passed away, we were on our own. The lights were turned off and there was no heat during the winter season. Everyone who shot dope in the neighborhood, my sister Tamar included, could be found in our basement. By this time, she was hanging out in the streets, running around any and everywhere she pleased, including truck stops. She was typically in the company of drug dealers, other dope feigns, and pimps.

There were various types of pimps in the 70s. There were what I call gorilla pimps. These types of pimps liked to control women. They made them sell their bodies through intimidation, including threats and acts of violence. Next, there was what I refer to as finesse pimps. These types talked women into prostituting for them and bringing them the money. Lastly, there were what I refer to as independent hustlers or OG-type pimps. These were guys who were dealers and shared drugs with the women they loved. Their women sold their bodies in exchange for drugs, and they protected them in return. Tamar fell for independent type.

When I was in my early 20's, I often went searching for Tamar on the streets and would ask around to see if anyone had seen her. When I found her, I would convince her to get into my car and would give her money. If anyone on the streets had a problem with her and I knew about it, they would have to answer to my brother John and me.

Part I: Birth of an Addict

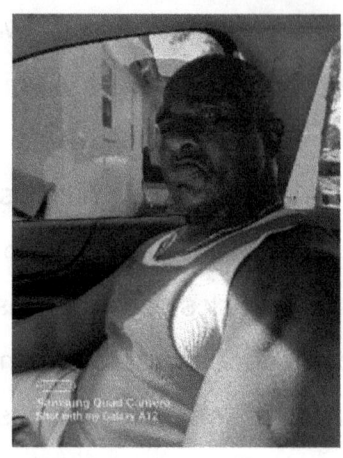

One day, John and I went searching for Tamar. We drove through skid row, an area saturated with bums, hobos, and drug addicts. We passed garbage cans people set afire to stay warm. We did not find her there. We searched through known dope houses and truck stops. Thankfully, we did not find her there either. Finally, we drove around the west side of Chicago near Washington & Paulina St., asking anyone who might've known her if they had seen her. We were informed that she was at Big Mike's house.

Big Mike was one of Tamar's boyfriends, one I referred to as a hustler-type pimp. When John and I pulled up, Tamar came running and screaming, stating Big Mike was trying to hurt her. John and I immediately sprang into action and began wailing on Big Mike. I busted his head open with my hand; there's a scar I still sport from that day. It wasn't until years later that I ran into Big Mike, and he told me that he respected Tamar and would've never hurt her. He stated that the day I tried to bash his head in believing he had harmed my sister, he was really trying to protect her. He explained that he was attempting to convince her not to leave the house so she wouldn't be out in the streets. I believed him when he shared this, but when it came to family, John and I were going to kick ass first and ask questions later. That's what we did on that day.

There was mutual respect amongst dope feigns and street people during these times. Tamar earned respect and people did not mess with her. One day, one of my sons and a nephew went over to Latrobe Homes and some guys from the neighborhood threatened to kill them. Tamar was good with what I like to refer to as street theatrics. She showed up to the scene with a brown paper bag and using her index finger, pretended to have a gun pointed at the young thugs. My son and nephew escaped unscathed.

Tamar was in and out of treatment a few times, trying to stay sober and turn her life around. When she was in her 30's, I convinced her to go into a drug treatment program at The Women's Treatment Center located on the Chicago's west side. She remained sober for about 7 years, but when she neared the age of 40, she got into an unhealthy romantic relationship and relapsed. By this time, her health had started failing and she never recovered.

One day, my sister Karla called to inform me that Tamar was in the hospital. One of my worst nightmares was to receive a call that Tamar had been hurt while she was out on the streets, but it was years of drug addiction and living the street life that had caught up

Part I: Birth of an Addict

with her. Her condition made her appear almost unrecognizable, she was tiny and frail. We spent as much time with her as we could, but she never left her hospital bed. She took her final breath there.

An article in Psychology Today reveals that a father's absence may have a significant impact on a young girl's sense of self. Without a father's presence and involvement, girls are more likely to be faced with diminished self-esteem, self-confidence, creativity, and sense of authority. They are more likely to become pregnant as teens, abuse illicit drugs, and drop out of high school.

Unfortunately, Tamar turned out to be another statistic. She was handed a raw deal in life, never afforded the protection and encouragement young girls need to pursue their dreams. She never graduated from high school. She became an addict at a very young age and had the first of four children by the age of 16. Her father, Robert Hardiman, was never around to check on her or to forge a bond with his baby girl as a father should. She never overcame the psychological trauma of whatever happened to her when she was a beautiful, shy 14-year-old girl left to fend for herself against predators.

In all honesty, there was once a time that I was embarrassed that Tamar was on the streets doing whatever deeds necessary to secure her next fix. But as I watched her die on her deathbed, I would've given my life to save her. By that time, it was too late.

The Glam Drug

Cocaine is a derivative of the coca plant native to South America, and was first introduced in the late 19th century, around 1860, by chemist Albert Neiman who recognized that when he isolated cocaine from coca leaves it made his tongue feel numb. It wasn't until about 20 years later that the medical community began using it as a powerful anesthetic. One of the first noted doctors to use the drug in this manner was an Australian ophthalmologist, Carl Koller, who began using the drug as a surgical anesthesia during cataract surgery, a painful process in which the alternative drugs were known to make patients nauseous.

  Long before cocaine became a symbol of urban decay, televised raids, or handcuffed Black men lined against squad cars, it lived a quieter life in America. It was once folded into the fabric of middle-class, offering to anxious housewives, businessmen, and weary travelers a modern pick-me-up. America did not yet know the shape of the storm it was ushering in. It only knew that it wanted to feel good, feel lighter, feel lifted from the weight of its own ambitions.

Part I: Birth of an Addict

History has its ironies. Few are as stark as the journey of cocaine. From the genteel parlors of white middle-class homes to the scarred streets of South-Central Los Angeles, from the bottles on pharmacy counters to the basements of government agencies quietly managing foreign wars; every movement of this powder tells a story. Not only stories of addiction but of America's racism, geography, opportunity, and who is deemed worthy of compassion or condemnation.

America's cocaine story is not linear. It is layered like sediment, each era pressing into the next, leaving an imprint on the landscape of a country that practices selective empathy. To understand why the nation responded with care to one era of drug use and with criminalization to another, one must follow the currents of power and whose suffering the country was willing to ignore.

If one walked into a well-appointed Victorian-style home in 1903— drapes, polished wood floors, portraits of stoic ancestors— one might find among the household remedies a small bottle of cocaine in the same cabinet as castor oil and peppermint tea. During those days, cocaine was sold as a nerve stimulant, a ladies' comfort, referred to as a modern medical wonder. Doctors prescribed it for many ailments: hysteria, melancholia, indigestion, toothaches, and the vague afflictions of women worn thin by domestic expectations.

Housewives—moral pillars of the emerging American middle class—weren't considered *drug users* of their time; they were

The Glam Drug

patients. Their quiet suffering was framed as noble, their anxieties as natural outcomes of duty. Cocaine slipped into this world with ease because it came not as a menace but as a remedy for the emotional labor of womanhood. Pharmaceutical companies, including early versions of the giants we know today, packaged it in delicate glass vials and elegant labels. Sears Roebuck catalogs offered not only cocaine kits but the means to inject them, delivered like any other household good. In 1886, pharmacist John Stith Pemberton released a fountain drink. This fountain drink, made of a concoction of cocaine and sugary syrup, was named Coca-Cola. Initially, the drink was only offered to middle class Whites.

There were no police raids on these homes. No mugshots. No moral panic. There was, instead, something far more revealing: silence. The drug was used by those whose whiteness insulated them from any scrutiny. Had it been predominantly taken by the agricultural workers, the immigrants in densely populated urban tenements, or the Black families emerging from Reconstruction, lawmakers might have reacted differently, as they had with opium when associated with Chinese laborers. But instead, cocaine resided among the protected. And protection changes everything.

When signs of addiction began to surface—shaking hands, restless nights, sudden need—the country's discussion turned not to criminality but pity for women who were deemed *overburdened and*

Part I: Birth of an Addict

overtired. Doctors spoke of "neurasthenia," of the demands placed on women's delicate constitutions.

It wasn't until 1899 that Coca-Cola decided to bottle its product, making it widely accessible to minorities and those considered lower class. Consequently, the company stopped using cocaine in its formula in 1903, which was believed to be a racially biased decision. The real issue was left unexplored: America's relationship to pleasure and escape, and whose suffering it deemed legitimate.

Because many people became addicted to cocaine for its euphoric effects and accidental overdose during surgery had skyrocketed, the medical community found safer alternatives and the U.S. Government began to criminalize its use. In 1914, some of the first drug legislation in the United States, The Harrison Narcotics Act of 1914, was enacted. Support for the law was also fueled by racial bias and claims that cocaine caused Black citizens who used the drug to become dangerous criminals.

By the mid-twentieth century, cocaine's public image dimmed, but the drug did not disappear. It traveled underground, drifting through jazz nightclubs lit by smoky, blue lights, the back rooms of Hollywood studios, and the lofts of bohemian artists. It became associated with creativity and endurance, often used by musicians seeking a spark through long nights and executives aiming to stay awake across transcontinental flights. Still, it was expensive—too

The Glam Drug

costly for most Americans, and therefore still shielded by the invisible protections of class.

A drug that lives among the privileged will rarely be seen as a threat to the nation. It will be merely a vice, a private indulgence, a secret that polite society keeps but chooses not to confront. Law enforcement paid attention, but they did not obsess. Newspapers mentioned cocaine only in whispers. Its users, often white and well-connected, did not serve time in overcrowded prisons. They saw doctor's offices, not courtrooms. They were described as troubled, not dangerous. This was the era in which the country deepened the caste line between behaviors considered sick and those considered criminal. Cocaine remained on the safe side of that divide … for a while.

In the 1970s, the country entered an age of spectacle. The economy expanded, corporate towers rose, and the culture of excess became both aspiration and entertainment. Cocaine, fine and white as snowfall, fit perfectly into the lifestyle of a nation drunk on ambition. It became the drug of advertising executives, Wall Street analysts, record producers, celebrities, and the many who wanted to feel as though they were part of that world. It was expensive enough to signal status, social enough to be shared at parties, and marketed—informally—as safe. Not addictive, people claimed. Pure. Elegant. Clean.

Part I: Birth of an Addict

In discos, from Studio 54 to Chicago's Rush Street, young professionals leaned over glass tables, slicing lines with platinum credit cards, laughing into the early morning as if the world was limitless. Hollywood actors and directors glamorized it, musicians sang about it, and magazine journalists referenced it with a wink. Cocaine became synonymous with status, success, energy, and productivity. The "Cadillac of drugs," some called it. The New York Times hailed it "the champagne of drugs".

I was around 14 years old when powdered cocaine use was popularized by celebrities and other people of substantial societal affluence and influence. It appeared in songs and popular movies such as *Superfly*.

During those days I idolized the famous comedian Richard Pryor, who admittedly abused cocaine. He incorporated the story of how he once set himself on fire while freebasing into his standup acts. I guess it was okay to laugh; he survived the ordeal and shared the details about it in his jokes. Some believe that the fire was a result of irrationality and impulsiveness caused by his drug use, while others believe that because he doused himself in high-proof rum first, it was a blatant suicide attempt. Either way, he survived the horrific ordeal and used the story of this painful moment in his life to share it with the world through his comedic acts and prospered from it. I erroneously perceived Richard's story of triumph as an endorsement that doing cocaine was cool. Even if it brought you down for a moment,

The Glam Drug

you could be resilient. I laughed listening to his standup act but would later realize it was no laughing matter.

The cool guys in my community – particularly the pimps and drug dealers – used cocaine to establish themselves as living a higher social status. Around their necks, they wore string-like necklaces with small capsules attached to them. Inside, a small serving of cocaine and a tiny spoon they'd use to snort it. A street guy who spent a lot of time around our family wore one too.

Gerrard Johnson, or G, was a drug dealer and my elder by about 6 years. He was a friend of my grandfather and uncles who treated me as a younger brother. I admired him. I was impressed by the way he carried himself. He sported nice clothes, gold chains, and drove Cadillacs. He spoke with authority and confidence, and I felt special in his presence.

He spent time talking to me about life, something I longed for and needed. "Knowledge is played not gave", he'd say. To this day, I don't know what he meant, but at the time it seemed profound.

Our talks usually took place in the confines of the family kitchen. It was a small space that was decorated with tan tiles, light green walls, and a round, glass table. G and I usually stood near the countertops talking for hours about my plans for the future. G would share the details of encounters with the many women he kept around or whatever illegal opportunities he was taking advantage of at that moment.

Part I: Birth of an Addict

One day he showed up to the house dressed to the nines as usual – red hoodie, red sweatpants, and red sneakers. The house was unusually quiet on this day. My uncles were in the basement and my grandmother tucked away in her bed.

G and I stood in the kitchen for one of our talks. He said to me, "Tio, you don't want to try heroin if you don't want to end up like your uncles, people will look down on you. But cocaine is the drug of the future." He opened his capsule and pulled out the tiny spoon and snorted. "Do you want to try?"

At this point in my life, I had too many burdens to bear. I was watching my grandmother wither away day-by-day. She had gone from weighing 180 pounds to weighing only 90 pounds. Her garments would be soaked in blood, so I took the responsibility of caring for her into my own hands. I carried her in my arms and into the bathroom to bathe her.

So, when G offered me cocaine, I thought, *why not?* At least I would feel good. I could use something to relieve my mind of all its troubles.

G unscrewed the tiny bottle lying around his neck, carefully extracted a small amount of the white, powdery substance using the tiny spoon inside, and slowly handed it to me. I reluctantly grabbed the spoon, put it up to my right nostril while holding my left nostril closed with my thumb. I inhaled deeply.

Part II: Life of an Addict

Magic Carpet

Cocaine has been referred to as numerous street names throughout the years: *coke, white boy, flake, nose candy, speedball, toot,* and *stardust,* to name a few. If I could've coined a new street name, I would've dubbed it, *magic carpet.* This describes my first hit.

I don't remember where G went after we stood there in my grandparents' kitchen and I took my first snort. Within a few minutes, I was mentally swept away by the rushing, euphoric high that took effect. Immediately, I was hooked.

I left the house and entered the heated Chicago streets, pacing back and forth, up and down with the confidence that I could conquer the world. I felt as if I were floating over the neighborhood. All the grimy people in my life and my troubles were left beneath me.

I was trying to calm my mind, but it continued to race. Prior to that moment, my drugs of choice were marijuana and alcohol; so, when I got back home later that evening, I smoked some marijuana and drank some Bacardi Rum. It wasn't enough.

I needed cocaine to function. Ironically, I never thought it would bring me down. I only saw it as a next-level, glamorous activity that would put people on notice that Tio Hardiman was on the come up. It also served as an antidepressant, although I didn't truly know the true meaning of depression.

Drugs back then were better quality; they took your mind off everything. I no longer wanted to feel sorry for myself, Tamar, or my

Part II: Life of an Addict

grandmother. I just wanted to feel numb. Unbeknownst to me, my emotional state was already there. Cocaine just helped me get my mental state there too.

The next day, I went to buy more cocaine from one of the neighborhood dealers. They wouldn't just sell to anyone; you had to be connected. I was known enough and had the gift of gab. That got me served.

The year was 1977 and twenty dollars bought enough supply to last for one day. I needed an income source. Since smoke detectors had just become law, I began stealing and reselling them to support my new habit.

After about 30 days, I was seriously spiraling. I now wore a cocaine capsule around my neck, too. It was summertime, and I met my friends Laphil Lewis, Roy, and Sherman (or June Bug as we called him) at our usual meeting spot – the railroad tracks which sat behind our homes. These guys were my best friends. Although we were now all 14 years old, we had grown up together from the age of 5.

We began our usual routine, going in and out of freight trains and walking down the tracks. I decided to let them in on my secret. I removed the tiny spoon from the capsule around my neck and demonstrated how to put it to use. As we walked, I shared the same lines that G dropped on me about cocaine being harmless and glamorous. I told them to check it out. They each took turns, one after the other, holding the spoon and snorting coke. We floated around the tracks, basking in our inebriated states.

"Stop where you are!" Because we weren't supposed to be trespassing on the tracks, railroad police were shouting at us through surrounding loudspeakers, abruptly interrupting our blissful vibes. We knew what to do. We all ran in opposite directions. This was a strategy we used so if they caught one of us, they wouldn't catch us all.

They began chasing after us in their cars and we ran downhill to avoid being on their path. I ran to my house and everyone else went their own separate ways. It was a close call. My adrenaline was rushing, and I was sweating profusely, but I was so happy and grateful to make it home that day.

The next day, my friends and I returned to the railroad tracks. We smoked marijuana, drank alcohol, and snorted cocaine. They were all hooked now, too.

Eventually, we all dropped out of high school although one of the teachers there, Mr. Smith, constantly lectured me about staying in school. In my case, not only had I lost interest, but some gang members were searching for me claiming that I stole Shirley White, one of their girlfriends. If I showed up to school, they were going to jump me or worse. I occupied the time I should've been in school hanging out and getting high with my friends. The streets became our school and addiction, our teacher.

Black Gold

By the age of 16, I was so deep into my addiction that I disassociated myself with the harsh realities of my environment. I had already been fantasizing about being in Hollywood since I was a kid, but I began trying to live as a Hollywood star.

Mom and George moved my siblings and I to the Henry Horner Housing Projects, one of the worst ghettos in Chicago at the time. "I am Black Gold", I told myself. I began referring to myself by the moniker, Black Gold. I sported an afro and always dressed in the finest linens I could afford. I was now driving Cadillac Fleetwoods, too.

Part II: Life of an Addict

In my mind, I was already an adult. I didn't want to live with Mom and George anymore. I lied about my age on a rental application to secure my own apartment.

Although we were underage, Roy, Phil, and I went to all the popular nightclubs. One of the most memorable clubs we loved to frequent was called Dingbat's. Dingbat's was located in downtown Chicago; it was the place to be. The well-known and affluent of Chicago as well as many celebrities congregated there for a good time. My friends and I lied about our ages to get in. Mr. T, who eventually became a household name from the popular television series, *The A Team*, was the bouncer there. He knew we were not of age but permitted our entry if we promised to stay out of trouble.

It was funny. Mr. T had a very calm demeanor but was quick to fight anybody who he felt was out of line. I once told a peer named Larry not to mess with Mr. T and he didn't believe me. We were onlookers as Mr. T broke him down in front of everybody. "I told you not to mess with him", I told Larry as I tried to contain my laughter.

The crowds at Dingbat's were always mixed with different races, genders, and ages. Even the gay crowd, or what we referred to as Geechee's in those days, were welcome. Most people who were gay hid it; men and women who were courageous enough to express their romantic or sexual interests in the same sex were ostracized. If they respected me for choosing heterosexuality and made no advances, I tried not to focus on their homosexuality. I was

Black Gold

Black Gold; I had an image to maintain and wasn't afraid to send a stern message.

A few years prior, my friends and I had been invited to smoke marijuana with a guy that was a few years older than us. We went down into his basement and then things got weird. He began baiting us; asking questions such as whether we like to try "different things" in life. Once we caught onto what he was attempting to throw at us, we beat him and trashed his place.

On the other hand, one of the boys in my community, Stevie, was flamboyantly gay. He tragically lost his life after some guys who had been released from prison moved next door to him and killed him in cold blood. They had dismembered him, leaving his body parts hanging on a clothesline in his backyard.

Homophobic in some instances, an advocate and hero in others. My friends and I confronted Stevie's killers; he did not deserve to die. This was a part of the persona I developed as Black Gold. And as far as Dingbat's was concerned, all were welcome. Most of the patrons respected one another.

One night I had a run in with the legend himself, Rick James. Rick and band members had put on a show in Chicago and came to the club afterwards, walking in like they owned the place. Rick floated through the crowd adorned in tight-fitted jeans stuffed down into his stacked boots, a tank top showing off his muscles and hairy chest,

Part II: Life of an Addict

and braids in his hair. My boys, Phil and Roy, were with me that day. I wanted to impress my girlfriend, Felicia, so I brought her too.

Rick James walked over to our table and boldly asked my girl to dance. She obliged. What the fuck was I supposed to do with that? It was Rick James!

He blew kisses at my girl, dipped her, grinded on her, and whispered in her ear as the two of them danced while I watched in a jealous rage. Felicia soon came back to our table and grabbed her purse. "This my girl; what the fuck you doing? I'm Black Gold!" I exclaimed. The Stone City band members jumped in my face. Knowing I didn't have the manpower to take them all, I watched as Felicia left the club with Rick James that night.

"Rick, I'm not going to buy no more of your records!" I yelled after them as they walked towards the exit. I haven't seen Felicia since.

That night, I met a girl named Evette. From that union, my first son was born. I was 16 years old. We had a second son when I turned 19.

Rock Bottom

From my early teens through my early twenties, I was a functioning drug addict. I abused a combination of drugs: I snorted cocaine and tac (I don't know exactly what tac was), smoked marijuana, drank alcohol, and took pills we called black beauties which were also known as speed. I found myself constantly chasing a high, wanting to escape reality. The persona of Black Gold along with drug use were attempts to mask the impacts from the unaddressed trauma I had experienced earlier on in life.

One day as I ran the Chicago streets, I decided to stop at one of my play auntie's apartments. Her name was Toot, and she shared space with her half-brother, Bud. Somehow, drug addicts knew how to find each other; Bud and Toot were also drug addicts.

While in their apartment, they pulled out a device that resembled a fire extinguisher. Toot held it to my lips and instructed me to pull in smoke and hold it for a few seconds. That was it! I felt as if I was floating around on a magic carpet again. This was the high I had been chasing but couldn't seem to achieve.

I was on cloud nine for about one minute, then experienced a crash landing. In an instant, I graduated from snorting cocaine to freebasing, and I was now stuck chasing that high. This brought me to my knees.

Freebasing is not to be confused with crack cocaine use popularized in the early 1980's. There are some differences between

Part II: Life of an Addict

the two. Freebasing involves using ether to free cocaine's chemical makeup or its "base" – hydrochloride and alkaloid – to free it from any additives or impurities. A heating source such as a lighter or torch is then used to heat the chemicals and inhale the vapors. The process makes the drug even more addictive, and this method of use is ten times more dangerous; ether is a highly flammable substance. Crack cocaine, just as destructive and highly addictive, is a crystalized form of powdered cocaine that is produced by boiling down and dissolving powdered cocaine using water and ammonia until it becomes a solid which can be broken into pieces, or "rocks", and smoked.

Once I was taught to freebase, I began chasing the feeling of that first high. I went from being a functioning addict to a homeless one. I went from wearing nice clothes and driving fancy cars to not having a car at all, running in and out of dope houses purchasing and smoking cocaine. Yet, I still had delusions of grandeur.

Rock Bottom

Sammy Rice was a friend and co-worker who I had met while working at Newark Electronics. We had addiction and our love for beautiful women in common. Whenever we got paid on Thursdays, we took our earnings and spent it on cocaine. After our Thursday binges, we were penniless and never made it to work on Fridays.

One day we had smoked all our money up and Sammy went into his bedroom with his woman, Vera. I heard their moans and whispers as they made love. At that moment, the effects from my high were waning; I began to experience dry mouth and paranoia. I knocked on the bedroom door and asked Sammy if I could make love to Vera too. Sammy put on his pants and grabbed his pistol. He confronted me and let off a warning shot in the air. He told me to get my crazy ass the fuck out of his house. I ran down the street and never returned.

Going into guys' houses and making love to their women was a habit I had developed in my 20's. I got a rush from it and wanted to prove I was a lady's man. One day I was at a man's house making love to his woman while he was away, and he unexpectedly came home early. I blocked the door with a chest of drawers and continued making love to her as he knocked. When I knew it was only a matter of time before he would force his way inside, I tied a sheet around my waste and attached it to a heater. I then jumped out of a 2-story building to escape. He chased me down the street; I ran from him but laughed at the same time. I felt untouchable.

Part II: Life of an Addict

But on this day, I was a far cry from that 20-year-old. I was living on the streets chasing the fleeting high I had experienced after freebasing for the first time. Before I had lost my apartment, I sold everything in it to support my habit. A drug dealer purchased my furniture, and I had given him everything except two chairs. He threw a brick in my window because I kept the chairs. Eventually, I sold my car too and was evicted from my apartment for failure to pay rent. I couldn't hold a job either; chasing that high became my life's mission.

One day, while I was in a dope house dressed like my idols, all green everything down to the underwear and still thinking I was the man, I became dizzy and collapsed. Someone had sold me some synthetic drugs that almost killed me. A few of the dealers walked me around the block and gave me water to drink. That saved my life.

I had no appetite for food and was extremely weak. Food was always secondary to getting high. It was an afterthought. I did not have an appetite at all unless I was sober.

There were many times that I left the dope house with nowhere to go lay my head. This was the worst feeling, the longest walk. Somehow, I met women during my addiction that allowed me to stay with them from time to time. They'd give me money and feed me, ensuring I ate enough to remain a healthy weight. They'd eventually get fed up and kick me to the curve, but I know to this day that owe those women my life.

Rock Bottom

I tried to stay away from family; I was embarrassed about what my life had become. My sister was married to Henry "June Bug" Brown, a gang chief in the Henry Horner Projects. I admired and respected him. I didn't want to bring shame to him either; I definitely did not want him to see me at the height of my addiction.

All those years I was striving to become a Hollywood star and looked down on my uncles for being heroin addicts. Yet here I stood on the streets of Chicago homeless. Strung out.

I no longer idolized Richard Pryor but resented him; I blamed him for my addiction. Although I had never met him, I somehow felt connected to him because we both were raised around drugs and prostitutes. He was a wealthy guy, and I was just another brother from the hood; but cocaine took us both down.

Part II: Life of an Addict

Dope houses were extremely crowded places during those times. If an addict overdosed there, their body would be thrown on the street like garbage. I wanted to avoid that at all costs.

One time I was getting high in a dope house on Chicago Ave and St. Louis St. I brought a woman along with me and I carved out a place in a bedroom closet for us to get high. My lady friend began performing oral sex on me while I was preparing to smoke. She asked for a hit and when I handed the torch to her, she burnt her entire forehead and set her hair on fire. I doused the flames with some water and put her out of the closet. She was distracting me.

I've always had the gift of gab, and it worked in my favor. I used it to con my way into free supply. I once pretended I was Muslim to relate to a drug dealer named Eddie who was a Muslim. He ran a dope house on Laverne & Adams Street. Eddie's gatekeeper was a guy named Big Red.

Rock Bottom

I did not know Big Red but told Eddie that he was my cousin. Eddie gave me $500 credit and when he called Big Red to verify our connection, Big Red said, "I don't know him but tell him to stay there until I get back." I left and avoided them both at all costs.

Cocaine addicts are resourceful, conniving people. I learned many tricks of the trade through observation. Who knew you could preserve and smoke cocaine residue? When there appeared to be nothing left in the pipe, I witnessed other addicts apply heat to a small amount of residue left at the bottom of it until it became liquid and spread the residue onto a mirror until it dried. Using a razor blade, they scraped the dried residue off the mirror and smoked it. Some even pretended to lose the cocaine, smearing some on the wall for later. Others preserved undetectable amounts under their fingernails to smoke to themselves. I called them cocaine scientists.

Some acts that addicts were forced to do, especially women, were unthinkable. I knew a man named Greg who was a wannabe pimp and drug dealer. He had a perm in his hair and always wore fur coats. He was my cousin Rodney's best friend, and he reminded me of one of the members of the singing group Switch.

One day Rodney and I dropped in on Greg. He had a lady there with him at the time. I cannot recall exactly what she did to piss him off, but Greg did something to her that was most disgusting and degrading while we were there. He placed a piece of shit on a slice

Part II: Life of an Addict

of bread and made the lady eat it. I couldn't stomach it; I knocked the sandwich out of her hand onto the floor.

Eventually, Greg received his karma. The lady's brother was a psychopath. One day as Greg was leaving his apartment building, her brother split his head open with a jack hammer, disfiguring Gregs face for the rest of his life.

I never did anything to completely compromise my values in exchange for drugs, but I witnessed unimaginable, dehumanizing acts such as these regularly. The trauma I had witnessed, along with chasing the high, eventually wore me down. I became so broke that I didn't want any money. I knew that money wasn't going to change my circumstances.

During this period of my life, my friends and I had some good times, but many more bad ones. Phil ended up in the penitentiary and my former neighbor Sherman moved to Mississippi. I lost contact with Roy but later learned that he did not shake the stronghold of addiction. He took his own life while in his early thirties, the mother of his child had left him.

I hit rock bottom on November 20, 1990, at the age of 26. I was homeless and my appearance was as if I was stuck in a time warp. I still had a 1970's afro. It was 4:30am and my cousin Artie and I were hanging out in the west side of Chicago near Central Park and Chicago Ave. The temperature was mild for a Chicago's winters night. As Artie and I spoke, he pulled a pack of Hogshead cheese and crackers from his back pocket with no intention of sharing it with me. We got into an argument because I demanded that he share, and we began to fist fight. Artie said that I had gone too far and needed to go into treatment. I began to reflect.

My circumstances could've led me into a situation in which, like so many others, I was left for dead stewing in my own waste, but I somehow knew that wasn't God's plan for me. I didn't even know how it felt to be sober anymore. I hadn't faced life with a clear head since my preteens, but I knew I wanted to get off the streets and rise above drug addiction.

A burning desire to change my life entered my being. A calmness came over me. I wanted to make myself, my deceased relatives who were watching over me, and my remaining siblings proud.

Part II: Life of an Addict

Part III: Death of an Addict

Giving Up Addiction

You might've heard that the first step to conquering addiction is to admit you have a problem. This is accurate. I had thought about entering treatment before, but somehow Artie's words penetrated my soul that night. He dropped me off at Westlake Memorial Hospital located in Melrose Park, Illinois where I signed into their substance abuse treatment program.

The first few days were the worst. I couldn't sleep. I was going through withdrawal and hung from the bunkbed like a monkey.

There were about 30 of us in the program. I had to establish rank there amongst the other patients to ensure they knew I wasn't one they were going to try to walk over and take advantage of. I

Part III: Death of an Addict

observed their interactions to understand who was considered top dog.

One of the patients was a man who was about 7 feet, 2 inches tall. During one of those first nights, He took all the sandwiches, which had been made for us all to consume, out of the refrigerator and stored them in his room. I confronted him; I told him he needed to 'come up off some of those sandwiches.'

"What the fuck are you going to do?" He challenged. I stood there, not saying much but not backing down either. He handed me two sandwiches, and we remained amicable for the rest of my stay. I was later informed that he should have been a basketball star but had gotten strung out on drugs. Once he left the program, he relapsed and was caught throwing televisions off a hotel balcony.

After about a week, my mind was clear, and I was sober. This was one of the toughest moments of sobriety, facing my problems and the decisions I had made with a clear head. The life that I had been living began to flash before my eyes. I recounted how I had fallen into the trap of addiction and the memories of how I grew up in turmoil began to resurface. These memories brought back painful emotions, but it was a necessary process if I was committed to healing and beating addiction. Taking inventory of yourself and working through the guilt and shame is a part of the process.

I began to see myself for who I really was – a man who was clinging to his internal little boy who had grown up in a dysfunctional environment. A little boy with limited coping skills who had never received support for the trauma he had witnessed. A young man who navigated through carnage and chaos and had turned to drugs to mask the pain. A man whose first children were born while he was in the thick of an addiction who couldn't be present with them or their mother because he was strung out and in the streets.

The treatment model was a twelve-step program. Each day was a new day to declare sobriety from drugs and alcohol by working the steps. These essential steps included:

1. Admitting your powerlessness and that life had become unmanageable.
2. Believing that a Power greater than ourselves could restore us to sanity.
3. Turning our will and lives over to God as we understood him.
4. A searching and fearless inventory of ourselves.
5. Admitting to God, ourselves, and others the nature of our wrongs.
6. Being ready to have God remove our defects of character.
7. Humbling asking God to remove our shortcomings.
8. Creating a list of anyone we had wronged and becoming willing to make amends.
9. Making amends with those people unless doing so would cause injury.

Part III: Death of an Addict

10. Constantly being accountable for your actions, taking personal inventory and immediately admitting our wrongs.
11. Praying and meditating to God for His will for our lives and the courage to carry it out.
12. Carrying the message of recovery to others with substance abuse disorders and practicing the 12 steps in all our affairs.

Cliff was my first sponsor in the program. He was an older gentleman who helped me through these steps. The program had a duration of 30 days, but I stayed for 90; I wanted to have a plan once I left so my sobriety would not be deterred; I didn't want to relapse.

After completing residential treatment, I continued attending Narcotics Anonymous meetings for many more years. I used the talents I possessed as Black Gold to better the lives of those around me.

My creativity returned to me, and I began hosting clean and sober parties under the business name X Man Productions. These parties were designed to enable addicts the opportunity to enjoy nightlife without the influences of drugs and alcohol around them. They were alternatives to regular lounges and nightclubs. Instead of alcohol, we served pop, water, and Mystic (a popular juice beverage during those times). I also produced comedy shows and stage plays.

One of my proudest accomplishments was that I opened a women's recovery house in honor of my sister Tamar, assisting about 50 women who endeavored to turn their lives around. This became a profitable business; I collected rent from them. I must however admit, although my behavior changed, my mental capacity had not. I was still obsessed with Fleetwood Cadillacs and had romantic involvement with some of the women.

A few years after becoming sober, I married my first wife, a woman who was not the mother of any of my children. Infatuated with her curves and beauty, I was about 30 years old at the time and had married her out of lust. She was a hot commodity amongst other men, so I had to have her.

There were initial signs that our relationship would be doomed from the start. On our wedding day, the cake fell on the floor. Although I saw it as a bad omen, I ignored it.

Eventually, it did not matter how beautiful I thought she was. Relationships based on lust will only last until the sexual urges run their course. It is then that the masks come off, and people's true characters are revealed. Our marriage only lasted for about three years. Because I had not yet resolved the childhood issues, including the detachment I experienced with my mother, and I didn't remain loyal. I was back to womanizing and began seeing other women.

Although I was now clean and sober, these issues remained constant concerns until I had the courage to face them. I have now been clean and sober for more than 30 years. I am grateful that I was spared some of the destruction I have seen others succumb to throughout the years: terminal illnesses, disability, dismemberment, and death.

Each new day I get to open my eyes is a gift, and I realize that the twelve steps I learned in the drug treatment facility can help any of us navigate through challenges in different areas of our lives. The twelve steps are universal and can serve as a moral compass. They can also be used to help us heal from years of trauma.

Step one is admitting your powerlessness over addiction. Not everyone is addicted to drugs. Some people are addicted to lying, some people are addicted to gambling, others are addicted to sex, some are addicted to stealing, and the list goes on. Admitting powerlessness over addictions and life's circumstances beyond your control will make you feel as though the weight of the world has been lifted from your shoulders.

Step two deals with restoring some form of clearer thinking so you can access higher levels of consciousness. Remember, insanity is doing the same thing but expecting a different result. Most people don't want to admit that they have been living in insanity, but life won't get better if we do not recognize our thought patterns, how they affect our behavior, and choose healthier, more productive thoughts and behaviors.

Step three is about deciding to turn your life and will over to a higher power. Some people say that religion is for people who do not want to go to hell and spirituality is for people who have been to hell and don't want to return; therefore, this step does not encourage you to subscribe to any particular religion. It's more so about developing a harmonious relationship with the Universe. We can all use a little faith. Rome was not built in a day.

Step four encourages us to take moral inventory of ourselves and to own the decisions we've made. This internal evaluation is the key to ongoing happiness. Many of us look good on the outside but continue to struggle on the inside. When you take moral inventory with a sponsor and begin the process of examining your assets and liabilities, you will begin to prioritize what you need to work on to become a better you. You can unlearn negative behaviors. We must shed the old ways to become new again.

Step five delves into the exact nature of our wrongdoing. We must take a deeper look into behavioral patterns that have been detrimental to others and ourselves. This is a golden opportunity to work with a professional to help process some of your darkest secrets. The truth can set you free! Although many of us are reluctant to share what we consider private affairs, it is essential for our growth. We should share more often because when we don't deal with our innermost issues, our thinking and decision making can be clouded. Hurt people oftentimes hurt other people. This is what happens when we do not confront the exact nature of our wrongs. It's like washing and putting a shiny wax coating on the outside of your car but leaving

Part III: Death of an Addict

the inside filthy with garbage. To become free of our past we must accept our transgressions and pay it forward by helping others.

Step 6 helps us to address our unchecked character defects. Left unaddressed, these defects can rob us of the benefits of ongoing recovery. Drugs are only a symptom of the real problem. These defects may present in many different forms such as lying, stealing, being unfaithful, excessive gambling, etc. A sponsor or professional can help you to discover and confront your character defects. It's all about getting better. Do not overlook this step. Some people will struggle with their defects of character until they either defeat their most glaring defect or the defect defeats them.

Step seven involves us asking God to help remove our shortcomings. Some degrees of sickness are graver than others. For example, some have treatable cancer, while others have terminal cancer. Shortcomings are more serious than one would ever know. It may appear on the surface that a person who constantly engages in behaviors that result in multiple stints of jailtime must like to be in jail. Otherwise, they would change their criminal behavior, wouldn't they? However, their main issue is really a result of a shortcoming in their thinking. That's why it is equally important not to judge people. We can address our shortcomings by working the twelve steps and taking things one day at a time instead of trying to deal with all issues in one or two days. We all fall short of the glory of God. Do your best not to allow your shortcomings to serve as a crutch to continue repeating negative behaviors. Work on yourself like your life depends on it and you will get better over time.

Step eight is all about restorative justice, unveiling wrongs and attempting to repair harm. Making amends with those who were once a part of the relationships you have destroyed. Taking a look at your wreckage from the past: broken promises, bad relationships, crimes against people, abandonment, family issues, taking people for granted, etc. and being accountable for them. Who have you harmed that you would be willing to make try to make whole? Write their names and move to step nine.

Step nine is an action step. It involves making direct amends with those you have harmed except if doing so would injure yourself or others. Your actions have led to resentment and pain, so this step is difficult. You cannot step on people and expect them to forget your transgressions. Just because you are willing to make amends does not mean the person you have harmed is willing to accept it. All you can do is try. Some of the people you have hurt may not ever forgive you. Making direct amends is for you and the person you harmed. If a person does not accept your willingness to make amends, then continue to pray for forgiveness. When we struggle with addiction, we often forget our responsibilities in life. Some of us have left our kids behind, have caused broken relationships, have unsettled debts, have engaged in devious behaviors against others, etc. We cannot expect a person to be forgiving right away after being taken advantage of year after year. People choose to forgive but not forget. One of the worst things to tell somebody is to *get over it*, assuming they can forgive and forget the pain of the past. It doesn't work that way for everybody, but the restorative justice model has been proven to help repair torn relationships. It is, however, a process that takes time.

Step ten involves taking a daily, personal inventory of your behavior and promptly admitting your mistakes. This step is all about character building and consistently addressing your wrong behavior. There is no margin for error with this step. You either choose to stay out of the hot seat or continue hurting people because your past addiction is always looking for a way to reenter your life. Sometimes we forget the behavioral issues that got us into trouble in the first place. This step encourages us to address even what we may feel are the simplest transgressions. If you hurt someone's feelings or tell a lie, immediately express to the person that you were wrong. This way you can avoid long-term resentment.

Through prayer and meditation, the eleventh step enables us to foster a transformative relationship with our higher power. This is essential in the recovery process. Many people make rash decisions, but meditating and seeking a relationship with a higher power before making big decisions can spare you a lifetime of suffering. Some of us have learned how to have more patience through this process. A sound spiritual foundation is better than having a pot of gold; you cannot pay for peace of mind. It's something earned through learning from your life experiences. Understanding what serves you and what doesn't will help you to avoid pitfalls. It's your job to protect your peace of mind. Prayer and meditation can be very helpful.

Step twelve occurs after our spiritual awakening. It is about giving back and helping others by sharing our experiences. One of the main reasons I decided to write this book was to share my experiences, strengths and hopes with people struggling with drug addiction worldwide. Humility is the key to ongoing recovery. You must give it away to keep it. Make no mistake, it was only by the grace of God that I pulled through my addiction.

Not all that glitters is gold. Go beyond your shiny surface and cleanse what lies within you. This will enable you to glow from the inside outside. Recovery is possible.

The Aftermath

As I transitioned to a sober lifestyle, I felt like I had been in a warzone. Pieces of my life were scattered everywhere, and I did not know where to begin picking up the pieces. In the world of addiction, it is easy to lose track of time. Days turn into weeks, weeks become months, months roll into years, and years into decades. Holidays, birthdays, children's milestones, and the deaths of loved ones all pass by. The recovering addict must, somehow, find a way to pick up the pieces and start anew.

As I became sober and my mind became clearer, I began to research the history of the drug epidemic in America. I was curious and wanted to uncover why predominantly Black neighborhoods saw the most devastation. During this process, I realized that, like so many others, I had been a willing participant in the demise of my own people and environment. I had been a pawn on America's chest board, a part of the diabolical plan to oppress the Black community.

I learned that drugs as powerful as cocaine don't remain static. It changes form, price, and geography. By the early 1980s, cocaine reached a point of overproduction. Colombian cartels were flooding the international market. What was once precious became plentiful. And faced with surplus, traffickers did what any business would; they innovated. They found a way to convert powder cocaine into small crystals that could be smoked, producing a quicker, more

Part III: Death of an Addict

intense high. The new product could be sold cheaply, in five- or ten-dollar increments, making it accessible to people who could never afford a hundred-dollar gram. They called it "rock," then crack—the sound it made when heated on makeshift pipes. And just like that, the drug that once lived in gated communities and mirrored nightclubs made its way into neighborhoods that had long been marginalized, disinvested, and overpoliced. Not because of moral decline or lack of willpower, but because this version of the drug was deliberately priced for the poor, and poor communities, especially predominately Black ones, had few economic buffers with which to resist.

Factories closed. Jobs had fled. Schools were underfunded. Supermarkets were replaced by liquor stores. Police officers replaced social workers. The stage was set for devastation. The same nation that had once pitied housewives and normalized the indulgence of executives had found a new target for its scorn.

South Central Los Angeles in the early 1980s was a place shaped by both resilience and abandonment. It was a community built by migrants of the Great Migration, who carried the memory of Jim Crow with them as they sought work in aircraft plants and defense factories that boomed during World War II. These were families who had moved West to escape the caste system of the South, only to find themselves placed in a different configuration of the same hierarchy. By the time crack entered the community, South

The Aftermath

Central was already navigating increased unemployment, aggressive police surveillance, and gang conflicts fueled by economic deprivation rather than inherent violence.

Then, into this landscape stepped a man who would become synonymous with the crack era. Ricky Donnell Ross, later known as Freeway Ricky, was not born into criminality. He was born into a geography of limited choices. Although he had the discipline of an athlete and was a talented tennis player, he could not read. He entered the drug trade not out of malice but out of pragmatism. When a mentor told him he would never qualify for a college scholarship because he was functionally illiterate, Ross found himself among the many who discovered that the legal economy has no place for them. Certain doors remained permanently closed for young Black men.

His rise was meteoric. He was disciplined, calm, methodical. Unlike many dealers, he reinvested every dollar, building a distribution network that spanned cities and states. But what truly made Ross a pivotal figure was not strategy; it was supply. Ross had access to cocaine in quantities and prices no one else could match. His supplier, Danilo Blandón, was not an ordinary trafficker but a Nicaraguan exile raising money for a U.S.-backed paramilitary group: the Contras, fighting the Sandinista government in a Cold War proxy conflict thousands of miles away.

Cocaine profits helped fund a war that the U.S. government publicly supported but couldn't legally finance directly. The result was

Part III: Death of an Addict

a pipeline from Central America to South Central. From geopolitics to street corners. Ross did not initially know these details. Few did. But the volume was undeniable. It allowed him to sell crack at prices so low that he edged out his competitors. The drug became widespread not only through desire, but market forces engineered by foreign policy.

For years, rumors circulated about the source of the cocaine that had inundated Black neighborhoods. But rumors are easy to dismiss when they come from communities the nation has been trained not to believe. That is until Gary Webb, a journalist for the *San Jose Mercury News*, pieced the fragments together. In 1996, Webb published *Dark Alliance*, a three-part series that alleged:

- Members of the CIA-connected Contra movement trafficked cocaine into the U.S.
- American intelligence agencies knew but failed to intervene.
- Cocaine sold by Contra operatives became the foundation of Freeway Ricky Ross's empire.
- The proceeds helped fund a war Americans were never told they were supporting in this way.

This news widely exploded across Black America. Church basements, barbershops, and college campuses all buzzed with confirmation of long-held suspicions: that the devastation in their communities was not merely a result of personal choice or inner-city pathology but was of international policy decisions made without regard for Black life.

Some mainstream media outlets attacked Webb's reporting, not because it was entirely wrong but because it challenged the authority of institutions that were considered untouchable. Yet later reports, including from the CIA's own Inspector General, verified the core truth: the CIA was aware that Contra allies were involved in cocaine trafficking and the agency did not stop them. Justice Department officials obstructed prosecutions.

Gary Webb lost his career for discovering and revealing the truth. He died in 2004, but history has been kinder to him than the institutions he challenged.

It takes a particular kind of blindness for a nation to criminalize one form of a drug while excusing another. But in a caste system, blindness is not an accident; it is a feature. Powder cocaine, used by the powerful, remained a symbol of wealth even at the height of the crack epidemic. Crack cocaine, used by the poor, became a symbol of moral collapse. Although the chemical difference between the two forms was minimal, their social differences were vast.

Congress passed the Anti-Drug Abuse Act of 1986, creating a sentencing disparity of 100-to-1. Five grams of crack triggered the same minimum and mandatory sentence as 500 grams of powder cocaine. Although the law did not mention race; it did not have to. Its impact spoke for itself.

Part III: Death of an Addict

The Reagan administration had started *The War on Drugs*, but, for me, addiction was an internal battle that only I could conquer. Understanding that the behaviors, attitudes, and habits that an addict chooses to adopt after treatment are critical, I began to examine myself. These factors help to determine the likelihood of success or relapse.

The people, places, thoughts and behavioral patterns that were once most comfortable to us become alluring traps, and we try to convince ourselves we are strong enough to escape their claws. But these snares of familiarity are deceptive; they could cause us to spiral and relapse. And the danger of a relapse is that we'll never know if we'll be afforded another opportunity to live through it.

Some of the work I needed to prepare was done during the recovery program, but the real test was to survive in the community as a sober man, not letting my family or myself down.

After the recovery program, I found that trying to discover the new me while assimilating into some sense of a normalcy was extremely challenging. I had almost spent my entire 20s chasing the cocaine high. I was 26 years old, and an entire decade had passed. I had lost a lot of time.

I had more children by this time, but my oldest sons had experienced my addiction at its peak. Although many parents find themselves separated from their children, I somehow maintained close relationships with my boys. I was determined to stay in contact

The Aftermath

with them because I didn't have my father and did not want to be like him. However, I still wasn't there for them as I should've been. Due to my behavior as an addict, there were times when the lights were out and I sold items from the home, causing an eventual estranged relationship with their mother. So, in my sobriety, I endeavored to reacquaint myself with them and other family members. And because I had become clean and sober, their mother dropped them off at my doorstep; they were 8 and 9 years old at the time. I was fortunate that God allowed me to reestablish a relationship with them. I raised them from that point on, and we have been solid ever since.

I initially found difficulty in finding an honest job that would pay me a living wage without a high school diploma, so I enrolled at Harold Washington City College, a community college that is a part of the City Colleges of Chicago system, to obtain a GED. The college is located in the downtown area and its campus spans about an acre.

Returning to school was a struggle. Although I was never illiterate, I had dropped out of school at the age of 15. I never realized until this point in my life how important writing skills were for entering the workforce. Not only couldn't I write well, but I struggled in math also. While I was out in the streets struggling through my addiction, I wasn't reading books and solving big math problems, other than the math necessary to count the money I needed to purchase my next hit and to ensure no one stole from me.

Part III: Death of an Addict

It's easy to mask your deficiencies with appearances, but the truth prevails over ignorance wrapped in name brand clothing when you open your mouth and begin to speak. I didn't want to mask my deficiencies; I wanted to improve. I befriended some young ladies at the school who were extremely patient and supportive. They helped me to improve in these subjects. LaShawn helped me to become a better writer, and Crystal assisted me in math. Because of them, I am better at writing and problem solving. I went on to earn a GED certificate. I did it for myself and to pay homage to my grandparents who had made sacrifices to send me to private school.

After earning my GED, I continued at Harold Washington City College in pursuit of an associate's degree in liberal arts. Professor Sammie Dortch, who taught sociology, provided the tutoring, support, and mentorship that I needed to succeed. I excelled in humanities, social sciences, and restorative justice courses, but I continued to struggle in math. What is usually a two-year journey for most students took me three years to complete. I had to repeat math courses 2-3 times before I finally passed.

Earning an associate's degree motivated me to continue my collegial pursuits. I enrolled at Northeastern University's Center for Inner City Studies in Chicago to obtain a bachelor's degree in liberal arts. The Center for Inner City Studies is named for Dr. Conrad Worrill, a pioneer in the fight to secure reparations for Black people in the United States. I had no idea how my studies there would have such a significant impact on my life. By this time, I was married to Allison. Allison was highly esteemed amongst her peers, distinguished and accomplished. With her by my side, I was better prepared to excel further than I had ever imagined.

Through coursework and lectures of Professor John Starks and others, I studied world history on a deeper level and understood the philosophical constructs of the Roman Empire and the teachings of Confucious. We immersed ourselves in literature, conducting comparative analyses of Eastern World Thought versus Western World Thought. I discovered that my African ancestors had a rich history that began far before slavery. They lived off the land before colonization and embraced each other as one. The depiction of African savages they wanted us to believe were far from the truth.

I became obsessed with studying Shaka Zulu, The Black Panther Party, and Malcom X; they became my heroes. As Malcolm X went to Mecca and returned enlightened, my mind was also expanded. I had studied almost 30 countries by graduation, and I became more conscious of who I was meant to be and the type of person I wanted to become. I earned a 3.8 GPA and dedicated this graduation to my grandparents also.

I did not want to stop the momentum of the success that I was experiencing; I was intrigued by the wealth of knowledge that I had attained. I had already proven to myself and the naysayers that I could conquer anything; so, once I completed my bachelor's program,

Part III: Death of an Addict

I remained at Northeastern University's Center for Inner City Studies and enrolled in their master's degree program. During my studies, I learned more about social stratification systems. I read the book *The Psychological Chains of Slavery* by Dr. Na'im Akbar, which revealed that the slave master's mission was to miseducate and dehumanize their captives so they could stay in control, using tactics such as rape to strip men of their pride and manhood, women of their virtue and dignity.

I began studying Black world leaders which boosted my confidence and revolutionary mindset. The word revolutionary is often misunderstood and is typically attached to people who are trying to overthrow governments or other extremist behaviors. But truly, the word means *freeing of the mind*.

Despite our history of enslavement, our people are still some of the most brilliant minds in the world; we are resilient. I am resilient and so are countless others who have suffered trauma, fallen into the street life, and found a way out.

The curriculum I mastered and the paths I crossed helped me to become a better man. I graduated with a master's degree in inner city studies. I could not have done it without the support of family and mentors such as professors Henry English, Joseph Levi, Robert Starks, Howard Saffold, Andy Thompson, and Lance Williams, who all were profound influences. Following in their footsteps, I accepted

The Aftermath

an opportunity to pour into students at North Pride University, where I currently teach courses in criminal justice and urban studies.

Tracing My Roots

When a person emerges from addiction, or from any life that has fractured their sense of self, the question of identity becomes urgent. Sobriety cleared enough space in my mind for the silence to speak. In it, I heard a call I could no longer ignore: *Know where you come from.* I took a test, through an organization called My Heritage DNA, and learned that I am 53 percent Nigerian, 7 percent Kenyan, and the rest 40 percent Eastern and Western European.

For most of my life, I carried my past like a shadow—long, shifting, and undefined. I knew the names of the people who raised me, but not the stories of the people who shaped them. I had inherited a culture but not a clear lineage.

Tracing my ancestry wasn't just about discovering relatives but also reclaiming the chapters stolen by time, migration, slavery, poverty, survival, and silence. As I dug into my roots, I began to understand that my struggles didn't start with me, and neither did my strength. The resilience that helped me fight my addiction came from generations of people who endured even greater battles.

Addiction had made me feel unworthy, disconnected, and unanchored. Ancestry did the opposite, it grounded me. The more I learned, I felt a sense of belonging. My ancestors were placing their hands on my shoulders and whispering, you come from fighters. Stand up.

Part III: Death of an Addict

Tracing my roots also changed my perspective on my relationship with my children. I had spent years believing the only thing I passed down to them was pain. But discovering my lineage reminded me that I was also passing down heritage, culture, and legacy. Understanding my ancestry gave me something addiction never could: A sense of purpose rooted in generations. A foundation strong enough to build a future on. A legacy worth living for.

Every Saturday morning at the PUSH (People United to Serve Humanity) forums, which are now called the Rainbow PUSH forums, Reverend Jesse Jackson Sr. would have the audience stand, and with fist raised repeat after him: "I am somebody!" Those are powerful words but knowing that you are somebody because you came from somebody else puts more power behind those words. It gives you reason to believe. Tracing your roots and knowing your ancestors gives you that knowledge, that permission to believe.

Every culture on earth has stories of origins passed down, ancestral homes spoken of migrations remembered. But for African Americans, that continuity was violently severed. The story became a single long sentence beginning with enslavement.

Human beings require continuity to understand themselves. Without it, the psyche will improvise, attempting to fill gaps, and build identity on fragments and instinct. Many African American families have done exactly that—preserved dignity, pride, and culture through oral tradition, music, faith, and community. But knowing where you come from in a literal sense—your people, your tribe, your region, your lineage—offers something deeper. It offers us rootedness, a grounding in time and place. It tells you that you did not simply appear on the plantation. You were someone before they took your name.

For much of African American history, genealogy felt like walking backward into a fog. Families could trace themselves to the 1880 census, maybe to 1870, the first federal record to list formerly enslaved people by name. But beyond that, the trail thinned, broke, and dissolved. The plantation stood like a granite wall at the edge of memory, blocking the way to whatever came before. It was the place where names were changed, families divided, and identities rewritten. For many generations, Black Americans believed that this barrier was permanent.

But something has shifted. Technology, once imagined as cold and clinical, has become a lantern in that fog. DNA testing, digital archives, and global databases have begun to stitch together the torn fabric of African American ancestry. What was once a story of erasure is slowly becoming a story of recovery. And with each discovery, the meaning of the word *roots* expands.

African Americans carried the collective wound of historical silence for hundreds of years. Unlike European Americans who could point to a town in Ireland or a village in Poland, most Black families could only point to a plantation—land they did not own, a name they did not choose, a past given to them without their consent. The

Part III: Death of an Addict

plantation represented both a physical location and a symbolic boundary. It marked the end of recorded identity for millions of Black people whose ancestors had been stripped of everything except their humanity. Elders would say, "We can only go back so far," and people accepted that not in sadness, but as truth.

But truth changes when tools change. DNA carries its own libraries that were never burned, never censored, never rewritten. It is a record of migrations, bloodlines, festering traumas, and ancient resilience. Inside each double helix is a map older than any plantation ledger. When an African American takes a DNA test today, it's not merely curious exploration. It is rebellion. It is restoration. It is reaching beyond the point where history attempted to end the story. Modern tests from organizations such as African Ancestry, 23andMe, and AncestryDNA can identify:

- Ethnic groups (Yoruba, Igbo, Akan, Mandinka, Fulani, Wolof, Mende, and dozens more)
- Geographic regions with surprising specificity
- Migration patterns that trace the movement of families before captivity
- Long-lost relatives, sometimes on other continents

This science is not perfect, but it is powerful. It offers what no plantation document can: the identity before the interruption. Receiving this information is such a spiritual experience. It shrinks the distance between present and past, once thought unreachable.

Tracing My Roots

Suddenly, a person born on the South Side of Chicago or in rural Mississippi can point to a several places across the ocean and say, "My people are from there." This is not mere imagination but biology confirming what history tried to erase.

If DNA is the heartbeat of the story, digital archives are its bone structure. Over the past twenty years, millions of documents once locked in dusty courthouses and fragile storage rooms have been digitized:

- The Freedmen's Bureau archives
- Slave schedules
- Plantation ledgers and wills
- Records of enslaved people who fought in the Civil War
- Church registers kept by Black pastors under threat
- Runaway slave advertisements
- Bills of sale, auction records, and emancipation papers

What makes these archives revolutionary is not only their availability, but their searchability. Names that once crumbled on paper now illuminate screens around the world. Families who disappeared from the record suddenly re-emerge.

A woman today might discover the plantation where her great-great-great-grandmother labored, then locate the ship that brought her from the Gold Coast, then match DNA with living relatives in Ghana. A man might learn that the African name he never knew has been preserved in a genetic signature shared by cousins

Part III: Death of an Addict

5,000 miles away. The plantation is no longer the last stop. It has become a middle chapter. A painful one, yes, but not the whole book.

Modern genealogy does more than give names. It gives context. Through DNA and archival research, African Americans are discovering:

- Tribal traditions.
- Languages their families once spoke.
- Skills trades enslaved people brought with them from Africa.
- Patterns of resistance.
- Cultural continuities: music, cooking, and spiritual practices that survived despite oppression.

When ancestry becomes specific, culture becomes richer. The vague idea of *African roots* becomes a living tapestry of real people from real places with real stories. You begin to understand that your ancestors were not simply enslaved; they were potters, blacksmiths, healers, drummers, farmers, warriors, queens, griots, merchants, and teachers. A people with lineage, not merely loss.

I felt an emotional weight reconnecting with my lost history. It felt as if I was coming home to a house I'd never seen. Others describe a feeling of grief—grief for centuries without a name, grief for ancestors whose stories were swallowed by silence. And along with the grief comes a healing, slow but undeniable.

DNA results and archival documents cannot undo the past, but they can restore belonging. They give descendants a chance to

speak the names of peoples and nations that slavery attempted to erase. For many African Americans, tracing ancestry becomes:
- A reclaiming of self
- A rewriting of identity
- A rebirth of pride
- A grounding in something older and deeper than the American narrative of survival
- A wound that always seemed too wide now healing

The field is still expanding. Scientists and historians are building massive African DNA reference panels. African countries are digitizing older records. Anthropologists are collaborating with Black genealogists to map migration routes and cultural histories once inaccessible. Some predict that within a generation, many African Americans will be able to trace their maternal or paternal lines back 300 to 500 years with clarity that was unimaginable even twenty years ago. Each year the gap narrows. Each discovery pushes the plantation further into its rightful place: not a beginning, but a rupture that can be bridged.

Technology does not heal everything. But it is giving African Americans something priceless: A past that can be known. A lineage that can be named. A story that can be owned. And for a people whose history was built on forced forgetting, this new era of remembering is nothing short of revolutionary.

Part III: Death of an Addict

There is a moment many African Americans experience when they open their DNA results or confront a newly digitized record of an ancestor: a trembling recognition, a breath caught between disbelief and belonging. It is a moment older than the individual and larger than the science. It is the soul remembering itself. Tracing roots is more than genealogy. It is emotional archaeology. It is spiritual recovery. It is the reclamation of a story that was interrupted but never extinguished.

For centuries, Black Americans were carrying the burden of beginning their family histories at sites of trauma: plantations, slave quarters, and auction blocks. That history was real and it shaped generations, but it was never the whole story. And now, thanks to twenty-first-century tools, millions of African Americans are able to move past the point of rupture and discover the beauty, depth, and complexity that existed before bondage.

Historical erasure is a kind of psychological violence. When a group of people is told, explicitly or implicitly, "Your past does not matter," they live with an inherited sense of dislocation. This is part of the intergenerational trauma of slavery. Modern genealogy interrupts that erasure. It says:
- Your ancestors lived full lives before America.
- They had families, rituals, and languages.
- They were not anonymous.
- They were not lost.

Tracing My Roots

Reclaiming this knowledge helps heal a generational wound. It allows descendants to shift from a narrative of survival alone to the narratives of continuity, achievement, and resilience. For many, discovering African ethnic ties brings a sense of relief. The kind you feel when finally locating something you didn't know was missing.

Many spiritual traditions across the African diaspora share a common belief: ancestors walk with the living. They whisper through intuition, dreams, memory, and the quiet moments when something simply feels familiar. Many people describe this feeling as a sudden alignment when they learn their ethnic origins:

- A woman with a lifelong love for drumming learns she has Mende ancestry.
- A man drawn to palm symbolism discovers Yoruba bloodlines.
- Families that sing in close harmony learn they descend from the Wolof people, known for vocal traditions.

These moments feel less like new information and more like recognition. It is as if the ancestors say, "Yes. That's us. You've found your way home." Genealogy offers a way to expand the narrative:

- Who were the first ancestors to arrive in North America?
- What African tribe or ethnic group did the maternal line come from?
- What skills, crafts, or spiritual traditions were passed down?
- Who resisted? Who survived? Who carried the family forward?

Part III: Death of an Addict

The answers to these questions enable a fragmented family story to become whole again. Parents can explain to children that their family did not begin in bondage; it continued through it. This shift changes how generations see themselves. It strengthens identity. It builds pride. It affirms worth.

Tracing one's roots does not erase the brutality of slavery. In fact, it sometimes uncovers moments of profound pain:
- Records of children separated from their mothers.
- Names of enslaved ancestors listed as property.
- Wills that distribute human beings alongside cattle.
- Signs of physical or sexual trauma.

These discoveries can be heavy and can trigger deep sadness, anger, or grief. But they also provide clarity about what your ancestors endured and overcame, adding depth to your understanding of their suffering makes cultural survival even more miraculous.

African Americans frequently discover cousins in Nigeria, Ghana, Sierra Leone, Cameroon, Guinea, Benin, Liberia, Senegal, and more. Some travel back to ancestral homelands and experience a feeling that defies logic; something like recognition in a place they have never visited. Others form relationships with cousins abroad, building bridges across oceans that slavery once tried to widen forever. These connections are not merely biological; they are cultural and emotional reunions.

Tracing My Roots

For 400 years, African Americans had their stories told about them, not by them. Plantation owners kept the records. Census takers misspelled names. Court clerks reduced people to race codes. Historians wrote from the perspective of the powerful. But DNA and digitized archives change that dynamic. Black descendants are now able to tell their own family stories, correct historical omissions, reclaim African identities, build genealogies once thought impossible, and preserve history for generations to come.

Ancestry is not just history, but power—cultural, emotional, and intellectual power. When a person knows where they come from, the world feels a little less rootless, and the future feels a little less uncertain. Identity grows stronger. Purpose grows clearer. Pride deepens. And beyond it stretches a vast ancestral landscape waiting to be known, remembered, and reclaimed.

Facing My Trauma

Tracing my roots did more than tell me where I came from. It showed me what had been living inside me all along. Long before I ever put cocaine in my body, long before addiction took hold, something had already been shaping how I moved through the world. Sobriety gave me clarity, but ancestry gave me the language to understand it.

For years I believed my addiction was the problem. If I could just stop using drugs, everything else would line up. And for a while, that belief carried me; but I've learned that early recovery is about survival. You're learning how to breathe again without chemicals, how to sit still without escaping, how to exist in your own skin. But once the chaos settles, something else shows up. Old feelings. Old fears. A constant tension that doesn't seem connected to anything happening in the moment. That's when I realized recovery wasn't just about what I was quitting but what I was finally willing to face.

Where I grew up, danger was normalized. So were addiction, violence, and silence. None of us possessed the language to identify these experiences as trauma back then; we kept it moving. We learned how to read rooms quickly. We learned the right times to speak and when to disappear. We learned not to expect safety, but only to prepare for imminent danger. Those lessons saved lives. They saved mine, but they also followed me into adulthood.

Part III: Death of an Addict

When I began tracing my ancestry, I started to see that my reactions didn't start with me; they had a history. My ancestors survived slavery, segregation, poverty, displacement, and constant threat. Their bodies also learned vigilance. Their nervous systems also learned endurance. They learned how to survive conditions that were never meant for human beings and passed that knowledge down.

Trauma doesn't just live in memory; it lives in posture and breath. In how quickly your heart races when nothing appears wrong. In how hard it is to rest even when rest is available. I had spent my life trying to outrun those sensations. Drugs slowed them down; alcohol dulled them. Cocaine made me feel powerful instead of afraid. Addiction became a shortcut to relief. But shortcuts always charge interest.

Recovery stripped away the numbing and left me face-to-face with myself. I had to sit anxiously instead of outrunning it. I had to feel grief instead of trying to bury it. I had to confront anger instead of disguising it as confidence or control. Tracing my roots helped me see that none of those emotions made me weak; but they made me human, a part of my heritage.

Slavery did not end cleanly; it left behind a trail of devastation. It fractured families, erased names, criminalized survival, and trained generations to expect danger. Even after emancipation, the threats continued. Jim Crow. Lynching. Redlining. Mass incarceration. Police

Facing My Trauma

violence. Every generation learned new ways to stay alert. New ways to protect themselves. New ways to harden. That hardness didn't disappear when laws changed; it became a part of family culture, a part of parenting and norms passed down without explanation.

I was raised to believe that men didn't shouldn't show fear and handled business themselves. That vulnerability was dangerous and asking for help meant exposing weakness. Those beliefs have been embedded in us throughout history. Addiction thrives in those conditions.

When I used drugs, I wasn't trying to destroy myself. I was trying to regulate myself. I was trying to calm a system that had never learned how to feel safe, but recovery forced me to build new tools: breathing, reflection, faith, honesty. Ancestry gave me compassion and helped me to understand why those tools were necessary in the first place.

Tracing my roots also forced me to grieve properly. Not just for my own losses, but for losses that predated me. Loss of language and land. Loss of continuity and protection. Those losses echoed in my life even when I couldn't name them.

Facing trauma means allowing yourself to feel grief without being consumed. It means acknowledging anger without becoming it. It means telling the truth without regretting it. Recovery taught me that facing pain doesn't kill you, running from it does. As I learned more about my lineage, I began to understand that I wasn't just the

Part III: Death of an Addict

descendant of trauma. I was also the descendant of resilience. My people survived the unimaginable and still created families, culture, music, faith, and meaning. That resilience lived in me too, even when I had forgotten it.

Sobriety gave me access to my life, while tracing my roots gave me access to my humanity. I stopped seeing myself as broken and started seeing myself as carrying unfinished business. Healing wasn't about erasing the past but integrating it, understanding it, and honoring it without being ruled by it. This understanding changed how I viewed recovery. My sobriety wasn't just about staying clean. It was about restoring balance—to myself and to the generations connected to me. When one person heals, it ripples outward. When one person learns to sit with discomfort instead of escaping it, that lesson travels. I began to see my recovery as part of a longer story; one my ancestors never got the chance to finish.

That realization changed how I carried myself. It gave meaning to my pain without glorifying it. It gave my survival purpose without ego. It reminded me that healing is not selfish, it is ancestral work.

Tracing my roots didn't give me all the answers, but it gave me the right questions. And it gave me the courage to stop running from them. By the time I understood what tracing my roots had revealed, I could no longer separate my addiction from my history.

The drugs were never the beginning of the story. They were the response. Recovery wasn't just about stopping—it was about reckoning. What followed was the hardest work I had ever done: learning how to break cycles that had been in motion long before I was born.

When you're breaking generational cycles, there are no big announcements. There are no applause or ceremonies. It happens quietly, inside decisions no one else sees. It happens when you choose to conscious responses instead of knee-jerk reactions. When you choose honesty instead of avoidance. When you choose healing instead of repetition.

For generations, my family survived by adapting. Silence kept people alive. Toughness kept people respected. Hustling kept food on the table. But survival strategies don't always translate into healthy living. What protects you in one era can imprison you in another.

Addiction is often a signal that a cycle is demanding attention. It's the body bringing to your awareness that something has been left unresolved. When I entered recovery, I didn't just change my own trajectory but had interrupted a pattern that had been repeating itself in different forms for decades. That kind of interruption comes with resistance. Old voices don't disappear quietly. They question rest and mock vulnerability. They romanticize suffering. Breaking cycles means standing firm even when the old ways feel familiar.

One of the most difficult lessons I learned was that healing requires rest. Not collapse or escape but rest. The type that teaches

Part III: Death of an Addict

the nervous system safety. For people whose ancestors couldn't rest without risk, choosing rest is revolutionary.

Another lesson was learning to speak the truth without rage. Silence had protected my family for generations, but it had also hidden pain. Telling the truth allowed that pain to move instead of stagnating. Breaking cycles doesn't mean placing blame on previous generations; they did the best they could with what they had. My responsibility: do something different with my new-found knowledge.

Recovery gave me the opportunity to choose differently. To model something new. To show that strength can look like regulation instead of domination. That love can be steady instead of conditional. That masculinity can include tenderness without losing power.

Cycles don't break overnight or all at once. They require consistency in choice, accountability, repair, and presence. That's how they are weakened. My ancestors survived so I could stand here, and healing ensures that survival turns into something more. That is how cycles end. Not with noise but with intention.

Giving Back

In 1997, I landed my first professional mediation job at Bethel New Life as a community organizer. My role within the organization was to plan around community safety by establishing peace zones and creating buy-in with members of the community including, young men, ministers, and community leaders. While working there in 1998, I met a man named Dr. Gary Slutkin, an epidemiologist with the World Health Organization. Slutkin introduced me to the World Health Crisis Model, or Public Health Approach, for treating gun violence. In 1999, I joined his organization, CeaseFire.

I experienced tremendous success working for CeaseFire. During my tenure, I helped raise over 20 million dollars and played an integral role in building the organization and its materials. I also engaged in a lot of the grassroots mediation work that made the

Part III: Death of an Addict

organization evolve to a thriving, well sought-after force in mediating some of the most dangerous conflicts across Chicago. I once stood between the member of a violent street gang member's gun and his target, earning the moniker, "Mr. CeaseFire". My success encouraged me to begin my own organization, Violence Interrupters, in 2004 while still working with the CeaseFire organization.

Violence Interrupters is a nonprofit organization whose focus is to interrupt and reduce incidents of violence–murders, shootings, and robberies–that are a result of gang activity and retaliations by 25 to 40 percent in select cities across the United States. We currently employ about 100 individuals dedicated to eradicating street violence in their communities. Our aim is to prevent violence before it becomes imminent, focusing our attention on targeted areas. These targeted areas are identified by the Violence Interruption Steering Committee. We achieve this goal through our mission and purpose, which are centered around the following strategies: community outreach and education, programming for at-risk youth, retaliation prevention, and consistent presence. We focus our recruitment efforts on the middle and high school levels, engaging students who live in our designated hot spot areas to participate in focus group sessions that promote peace. We also spend quality time with them, making authentic connections to build trusting relationships.

Violence Interrupters meet with victims of violent crime to prevent any further acts of violence. We not only discuss their life decisions, but we also connect them to resources. This strategy has been instrumental in defusing potential incidents of homicide through retaliation. It is pertinent that our staff are active in the target areas to ensure the diffusion of any potential threats and instances of violence. We are consistently engaged with members of the community and strive to remain informed of current events. Building relationships coupled with this strategy is a main ingredient in our success.

Importantly, Violence Interrupters are adults who have lived the street life and understand how to influence our clients. Our staff has the capability of helping people who've been infected with violent thinking to cross the bridge before they're thrown into the deep water.

In 2008, Violence Interrupters was hired by The U.S. Humane Society to launch a program designed to end illegal dogfighting. We partnered with professional dog trainers to educate young men to treat animals humanely and hosted "Love Your Pet" shows. The End Dogfighting Program also served as a part of the rehabilitation efforts

Part III: Death of an Addict

of former NFL quarterback Michael Vick, who was convicted of heading an illegal dogfighting ring and was slated to be released, after serving 23 months in prison, the following July 2009.

It was reported that some of the dogs in Michael Vick's camp were fed gunpowder and put in dark cages. They were made to suffer and were physically abused. They were strung up by ropes to make them physically stronger. Pit bulls will fight to the death to please their masters. If they lost the fight and did not die from their wounds, some of them were drowned to death.

I personally worked with Vick and was surprised by his humble personality. He caught a plane to meet me in Chicago and never wanted me to rent a special car to transport him. He barely wanted people to know he was in the car with me.

Giving Back

During the 3-year period the program was in existence, Vick covered the financial obligations to rehabilitate the dogs that were in his camp including all medical bills. We also went to Capitol Hill in Washington, D.C. to speak to legislators. When we arrived there, the women swarmed around us. I was still so full of myself that I thought the women were there to see me, but they were there to see Vick.

Micheal Vick has a remarkable story of how you can lose it all and turn your life around with a second chance, just as I did when I decided to let go of drugs and alcohol. Vick eventually returned to the NFL after his release. Since retirement, he has continued a career in football as head coach at Norfolk State University.

From this experience, I gained a lot of respect for people who care for animals, especially animals that have experienced trauma. I also adopted some of the dogs through the Humane Society to aid in their recovery. I adopted pit bulls named Rocky, Roxy, Destiny and

Part III: Death of an Addict

Mona Lisa. These dogs had unique personalities and could be a handful.

Rocky bullied the other dogs when he first arrived. He had a very loud bark and would back them into corners. I found myself constantly chastising him. One day, while playing with Roxy, I fell in the yard and Rocky stood over me as if he knew he could attack me but had decided not to. I was grateful that he didn't, and we became best friends thereafter.

Another time the dogs ran away and were found hanging out on the south side, thanks to their microchips. They were brought back to me in police cruisers. Destiny's fur reeked of guilt; she wouldn't even look me in the face.

Mona Lisa was a survivor of dog fighting, as evidenced by the many scars she wore. She was afraid to come out of the bathroom and never wanted to leave my side. I sent her to Best Friends Animal Society in Utah where she was rehabilitated.

Violence is a learned behavior. This was the case for Michael Vick who grew up watching and participating in dog fighting. Most domestic abusers witnessed other perpetrators of domestic violence when they were children. The same is true for youth who participate in violent gang activity and sex trafficking.

Violence is a suffocating weed in the garden of this world that must be plucked out. I decided long ago that I would use my voice, knowledge and platform towards solutions. Violence must stop.

Giving Back

In 2013, the year I left the CeaseFire organization, Violence Interrupters was established as a not-for-profit entity. We have been making news headlines ever since and have received several nationally acclaimed accolades and awards. Violence Interrupters has also trained more than 50 partners in cities across the United States and the UK, held more than 200 peace circles, and mediated over 1,200 conflicts since our inception to the present. In 2004, the year Violence Interrupters was established and launched, the City of Chicago witnessed a 25% reduction in instances of homicide, the largest decrease they had seen in 30 years.

Our success caught the attention of Steve James, Director of the popular documentary *Hoop Dreams*, and Alex Kolowitz, Author of *There Are No Children Here*. They approached us wanting to film a documentary highlighting our work. In 2011, "The Interrupters" aired on PBS Frontline to a worldwide audience. The documentary was recognized with an Emmy award. This was a pivotal moment for our organization. People began visiting Chicago to learn more about the work of Violence Interrupters and we expanded services to other cities such as Baltimore, Memphis, Houston, Detroit, St. Louis, Philadelphia, and Minneapolis, and the Bronx, Harlem, Queens, and Brooklyn in New York. We also provided services internationally to the United Kingdom, the Middle East, and Africa. I was introduced to prominent people who were interested our work like Queen Noor of Jordan, Former Prime Minister David Cameron and Theresa May

Part III: Death of an Addict

from the UK, Former President Bill Clinton, Former First Lady Lara Bush, and other dignitaries across the world.

Top Left to Right: Former Police Chief James jackson and Former First Lady Laura Bush; Bottom Left to Right: Police Chief from the Netherlands, Former Prime Minister David Cameron, Queen Noor of Jordan

The Great Fall

Life has its ebbs and flows, its ups and downs. How we deal with the situations that are thrown at us and manage our emotions determines our character. Although the days of being an addict on the street were behind me, I was faced with other challenges that could have easily caused me to relapse, but I didn't.

By 2013, I had been married to my second wife, Allison, for 13 years. We met at a restaurant in 1999. I was about 36 years old at the time, and it was love at first sight. Allison was both beautiful and successful. She had a caramel complexion and a bright smile. She worked at the post office and drove a Mercedes Benz.

Allison and I were inseparable. Although we both had our own apartments, we once thought about giving them up and moving into a trailer home together. We just wanted to be together.

I believe she had a spiritual gift. I loved her but was never faithful to her or any other woman for that matter. I recall an instance in which I was about to have sex with another woman and Allison somehow knew. She called me on the phone 10 times, and I left without touching the other woman.

Our lives changed on May 31, 2013, while I was working as Director of CeaseFire. Allison and my daughter had gotten into a verbal altercation. I did not want to get in the middle of them, and although both Allison and I had both asked my daughter to go back

Part III: Death of an Addict

to her mother's house, she refused to leave. Allison and I also had a disagreement regarding the conflict.

Later that night, Allison attempted to extract my daughter from her bedroom. I intervened by grabbing Allison, preventing her from physically attacking my daughter, causing Allison to hit the floor. In the process, her lip was busted. I didn't realize at that moment that Allison had sustained any lacerations or bruises; I thought the incident was over.

The next morning, Allison got up, took a shower, and went down to the police station to file a report of assault and domestic violence against me. I was in disbelief; I had not intentionally harmed her but was simply trying to prevent a physical altercation between her and my daughter, two women whom I loved very much. I believe that Allison was upset because she might've thought that I had taken my daughter's side and didn't do enough to defend her stance.

Once she filed the report and brought the police back to our home to arrest me, the news channels were all over it. We made national news. Our lawn was flooded with reporters. I asked her, "Are you really going to go through with this?"

Domestic violence was prevalent in the community where I grew up. Both during my primitive years and as an adult, I witnessed countless acts of violence against both men and women. Although I did not personally witness it, members of our community knew that Hawk had once broken my mother's jaw. But this wasn't the example

The Great Fall

my grandparents had set for me. My grandfather never laid a finger on my grandmother.

I was occasionally a victim of domestic violence myself. One incident resulted in one of my girlfriends hitting me in the head with a cast iron skillet. I pushed her from me to defend myself and to avoid any additional blows, but that was the furthest I had ever gone putting my hands on a woman.

In my eyes, women were fragile creatures who were meant to be cherished. So, standing there with my living room facing my wife (the woman I adored) and the police, I was both outraged and confused. Allison couldn't look me in the face; she hid behind the officers and ignored me. A police officer said to me, "Your wife said you beat her up and we have to arrest you for domestic violence." They even returned to our home later because Allison had told them that I had guns in the house.

Initially, I wasn't aware of the magnitude of the consequences I was about to endure. I was escorted to the local Cook County lockup in Hillside, Illinois, and my experience there was surreal. The police chief immediately called the media, and my picture was plastered all over the news with the caption, "Man that promotes peace arrested for domestic violence." A small piece of fabric resembling aluminum foil was my blanket for the night, and I was permitted to call one family member.

Part III: Death of an Addict

The next morning, I was transported to the Maywood Court Building in Maywood, Illinois for an arraignment hearing. Bond was set at $20,000, but I wasn't even interested in posting bond. I became deeply depressed; the good reputation I had spent so many years building was destroyed. I saw a lot of sheriffs I knew from my work in the community and placed my hand on one of their shoulders. He blurted, "Get your hands off me, Mutha Fucker!"

After the hearing, I was transported to Cook County Jail and placed in the bull pin. The experience was dehumanizing. I was in a cell with about 25 people and one of them looked as if he was taking a shit on himself while in a heroin nod. I heard another guy whisper, "I think he works with the police." I immediately squashed that myth; I was not going to allow him to endanger my life spreading false information. I corrected him: "I work for CeaseFire. You're not going to put that label on me!" I didn't say much else; I learned that it was best not to talk a lot while there because you never knew who was listening and watching.

Next, I was taken through a classification assessment. Each detainee was classified as maximum, medium, or low risk. I was considered low risk. From there, I was escorted through a tunnel and taken into an area where I was instructed to remove my clothing so they could swap them out for a jail uniform. Before I was allowed to get dressed, a long swab was forced into my penis for a sexually transmitted disease screening.

The Great Fall

You were forced to turn over everything in your possession during processing, dignity included. One guy hid stacks of paper in his shoes and another attempted to hide a cell phone. I witnessed the guards go off on them! Next, each detainee was escorted to a tier based on their classifications and I settled in my cell for the night.

The next day, I was called down for court again. Before I went into the courtroom, I overheard one of the guards in holding pin speaking to another guard stating, "That's that Tio Hardiman. He's supposed to be keeping the peace but he's over there beating his wife".

As I entered the courtroom, I was overwhelmed by the number of news reporters present. By that time, a family member and some of the guys I had helped in the community had raised enough funds for the judge to release me on bail, but I wasn't ready to leave jail. I went back to the Kool Aid and bologna sandwich that was waiting for me. A guard named Laverne that I knew from the community checked on me periodically but wasn't allowed to speak to me.

As I ate my lunch, a younger man approached me and asked, "I look up to you, Man. What the fuck are you doing here?" I always saw myself as a positive example for the younger generation, so that stuck with me.

I had to find a way to redeem my name. I said to myself, "If I can survive drug addiction and my upbringing, I can overcome this". I was ready to be released.

Part III: Death of an Addict

Upon my release, I held a new press conference where I announced that I would be starting a domestic violence program. Allison and I got back together about a little over a month afterwards. I was fired from CeaseFire within 24 hours; the negative press was a big blot on the organization's record.

Later during the month of June, a status hearing was held, and Allison dropped all the charges. She wasn't coerced by anyone to do so; we both knew what really happened on the night in question and it was the right thing for her to do. I truly believe that her sisters might've encouraged her to press charges in the first place. They never liked me because they thought I was too slick to be with her.

My reputation still hadn't been restored. I went from wearing suits and ties every day and meeting with prime ministers all over the world before the incident to wearing sweats and t-shirts. I went from making $180k per year to bringing home $600 per month in unemployment wages; I had lost all my retirement savings. No one would hire me; my face was plastered all over the news as someone who beats women. I even attempted to apply for a job as a truck driver. During the interview, I was asked to put the truck I reverse and back it up. I got into my car and drove off, never to return.

My focus was still to find a way to recover my losses and repair my reputation. Doing so would take some planning and creativity. I've had to think outside the box all my life, so I knew the

The Great Fall

answer could be found within. It eventually came to me. I thought, *Fuck this, I'm running for governor!*

Hardiman for Governor

Illinois has had its share of colorful governors. There was a standing joke that you could get to prison quicker by being an Illinois governor than you could robbing banks. Whether a governor was corrupt or not, or whether he (there were no female Illinois governors in my lifetime – or ever, as far as I know) – whether he deserved a prison sentence often depended on which political party was making the decision. By no means do I have first-hand accounts of each Illinois governor that served in my lifetime. When Otto Kerner, Sam Shapiro, and Richard Ogilvie were serving their terms, of course I was much too young to know or care anything about politics. When Dan Walker was walking and ruling the state, I was too high to know or care. It wasn't until I began attending Northeastern Illinois' Center for Inner City Studies that my mentors such as Bob Starks, Andy Thompson, and Conrad Worrill piqued my interest in politics.

      Otto Kerner had progressive views back in those days when Jim Crow was exiting; Civil Rights was becoming a reality. He was known for expanding mental health services in Illinois and supporting civil rights legislation. He famously chaired the Kerner Commission which concluded that America was moving toward "two societies, one Black, one white – separate and unequal." But after leaving office and becoming a federal judge, he was convicted of bribery, conspiracy and tax fraud – charges that his proponents, especially the Black community, never accepted as true or fair, but rather

Part III: Death of an Addict

retaliation for his support of Black people and Black causes. Samuel Shapiro was more of an interim governor, serving only a year. Other than pushing for transparency and ethics reforms in response to the "Kerner scandal," he didn't really do anything notable as governor.

Richard Ogilvie was noted for bringing more modernized ideas to state government, expanding the public transportation system and introducing state income tax. The reaction to the state income tax was widely negative, which is why he lost his reelection bid in 1972.

Dan Walker lived up to his name, as he walked the breadth of the State of Illinois meeting voters during his campaign. If you asked anyone, they would say he was largely ineffective as a governor, and although he was a Democrat, he was disliked by both the Democrats and Republicans. Although he wasn't indicted or convicted while in office, years after leaving office he was convicted of bank fraud and served prison time.

Perhaps the best known and longest serving governor was James R. Thompson, known as "Big Jim." Unlike his predecessor who was unfavored, Governor Thompson was personally popular, well-liked by Democrats and Republicans alike. Although he was never charged with wrongdoing, he faced criticism for the growth of machine politics and patronage, and for failing to seriously confront systemic corruption.

The Black community's beef with Thompson was coopting the gambling policy, which had served as the economic engine of the

Black community until its illegality was strongly enforced. It became legalized as the Illinois State Lottery, an eventual multi-billion-dollar industry. Thompson served as Governor from 1977 until 1991, and the Illinois State Lottery was launched in 1978. He served fourteen years, leaving voluntarily after four full terms.

George Ryan, although a quiet-spoken man, made one of the greatest achievements in Illinois history by putting a moratorium on the death penalty. The powers that be never forgave him. After years of investigation, he was indicted and sentenced to prison.

Rod Blagojevich served as governor from 2003 to 2009. He hired more African Americans to important administrative positions than any governor previously or since his tenure. One of his most hated by some and loved by many actions was appointing Carolyn Adams, a Black woman, to the position of Superintendent over the multi-billion-dollar Illinois State Lottery. The ire of the opponents of that action grew immensely when Adams named a Black advertising agency, RJ Dale, Inc., as the agency of record overseeing all media-related transactions for the Lottery. Adams served in that position for seven years, until she died from breast cancer. Soon after her death, the Lottery was placed in the hands of a private organization. When Congressman Jesse Jackson, Jr., the son of Reverend Jesse L. Jackson, Sr., was indicted and imprisoned, it left a vacant seat in the US House of Representatives to be filled by a governor's appointee. Blagojevich was accused of soliciting bribes and openly trying to sell

Part III: Death of an Addict

the seat. In an FBI-recorded conversation, he was heard saying to his brother Robert, "This is golden." Blagojevich was impeached, and imprisoned.

Pat Quinn was appointed to fill Rod Blagovich's term, and he made a promise that he would not run for another term. A promise that was quickly broken.

I felt that Illinois needed and deserved an honest governor who cared about his constituency more than he cared about his personal wealth opportunities. I felt that the Illinois voters, especially African American voters, deserved a governor who cared about them. I had dreams, I had ideas, I had plans to make Illinois not only great, but crime-free through violence reduction and gun control.

By the time I decided to run for governor, Illinois had already taught its people to expect disappointment. Even the governors who escaped prosecution left behind financial wreckage they never had to repair. Illinois didn't just endure corruption; it learned to live with it.

Two days after my release from jail, I sat down for a previously scheduled interview with Channel 7. I had been addicted to media for years, long before the domestic violence incident put cameras on my lawn. I spoke with reporters and shared my side of the story. I proclaimed my innocence and announced that I would be the next governor of Illinois. It wasn't a calculated political maneuver; it was survival. I had lost my job, my income, my reputation, and nearly my family. Running for governor wasn't about ambition—it was about reclamation. I needed my name back.

I made the announcement in 2013. I launched my campaign in 2014. People laughed. My friends thought I was delusional and underqualified. A few said I had nerve, saying it out loud after what had just happened to me. But in a state where governors fell hard and often, my fall didn't feel disqualifying, it felt familiar. They did not know that I had always fantasized about running for Governor of Illinois or for President of the United States long before this moment. Since I was no longer working for the state, the timing aligned with my ambitions, and I was ready to move forward.

To be placed on the ballot, I collected 10,000 signatures. I had a campaign office in the Maywood community but worked much of the campaign out of my Cadillac Fleetwood. I did not have any money to run television campaign ads but was running a $1 million campaign with a $40,000 budget. I spoke to over 400,000 citizens

Part III: Death of an Addict

statewide, many of whom expressed that they had forgiven me for my involvement in the domestic violence incident. I told them not to check on me or feel sorry for me, but to check on my wife.

During my campaign, I made promises to make the streets of Chicago safer. I planned to achieve this by funding programs that aimed to reduce gun violence. This included expanding my domestic violence program, which had already saved the lives of 15 women. Additionally, I promised to lower taxes for the poor.

Let's be clear: I cared about the citizens, but my motive for running for office was to get back my name. To polish my tarnished reputation. By securing 125,500 votes (28.1% of the vote), I believe I achieved that.

I lost the governor's race to Pat Quin who eventually lost to billionaire Bruce Rauner. Rauner has gone down in history books as the worst governors the State of Illinois has ever had.

Allison and I tried to stay together, but it wasn't the same as it had been. We had been together for 14 years with no prior incidents.

We had filed for divorce from one another four times and canceled. A few years later, Allison went through with it. She divorced me. I felt faint on that day, and it took years before I was ready to accept it and move on.

The run for governor yielded some positive results but wasn't enough for me. I sued Fox News for $10 million for reporting that I was "convicted" of domestic violence. They tried to settle out of court, but my ego wouldn't allow it. They made me look bad in court; attempted to diminish my character by mentioning my prior bout with drug addiction. The case made it to the appellate court, but I lost the case. In hindsight, I should've accepted the settlement offer.

When you're riding high on the waves, remember that the low waves will come. When they do, you'd better know how to ride them, or they'll take you under.

I ran for Governor of Chicago again in 2018. My opponents were billionaire JB Pritzker, Chris Kennedy of The Kennedy Family, and Daniel Chris. I had neither funds amounting anywhere near the $170 million that JB Pritzker spent on his campaign nor the influential backing of the Kennedys, but I held my own. In the process, I learned that when you are running for a high-ranking office, you will be tested and tempted.

Part III: Death of an Addict

One day, three guys – two Black men and one White man – came to my house pretending to endorse me for the candidacy, but I knew better. I was suspicious from the start. Both their appearances and behavior were off-putting. One of the Black men wore a fake mustache, and I noticed the tiny, hidden camera in the White man's ballcap. The third man asked to use my bathroom and instructed me to check behind him when he came out. He had left $25,000 there. The money was not being offered as a friendly, supportive push; it came with a message: "Drop out of the race."

I was furious and so were my pit bulls, Rocky and Destiny. They began barking and growling at the men as I handed the money back. I also barked: "Each one of you get the fuck up out my house before I sick my dogs on you!"

The fact that I did not accept the money was a true testament that I had turned my life around. Even if I had a fleeting thought to accept it, I didn't even know how I would've lived with myself. I had come too far to go back to my old ways for $25,000. My freedom was worth much more; it was invaluable. That day, I chose to lead with integrity. I know that my grandparents would've been proud.

When you're riding high on the waves, remember that the low ones are coming. When they do, you'd better know how to ride them or they'll take you under.

Message to People Suffering from Drug Addiction

Addiction knows no race, creed, or color; it is a universal concern that affects us all. Millions of people are addicted to drugs in one form or another – rich people and poor people alike. However, there is a light at the end of the tunnel called recovery. Always remember, drugs are just a symptom of the main problem which has been impacting many different areas in your life. It could be the symptom of depression, dysfunctional family dynamics, peer pressure, loneliness, lack of a solid foundation, and many more personal issues that might have led you to become addicted.

The disease of addiction is like having a ball and chain wrapped around your foot everywhere you go. Although through 12-step programs and other treatment modalities, millions of people have chosen sobriety, remember that the recovery process is for those of you who want to recover, not for people who need recovery. Let me explain … You must become sick and tired of being sick and tired. You'll know that you're ready when you are willing to totally surrender. The only way to escape active addiction is letting go and letting God.

Once you become clean and sober, you will realize that using drugs served as an outlet to mask the real pain. It is very important to heal from the pain of the past. Failure to address past issues will oftentimes lead you to relapse on drugs again and again. Some of

Part III: Death of an Addict

you might've even already hit rock bottom on several occasions but will not admit defeat. Pride comes before the fall.

I've decided to tell my story as an effort to help others release themselves from the stronghold of addiction. If the pitfalls of life have not destroyed you completely, then you have an opportunity to build a stronger foundation. Because it's very easy to become complacent in life, it won't be easy. You must leave the past in the past but always keep the door of your past open a little to serve as a wake-up call and reminder of where you've come from. Never forget so you won't be tempted to go back there. Do your best to stay around positive people who are on the move. Success isn't always measured by financial wealth but can be as simple as having peace of mind.

Try not to feel defeated when things are not going your way. Remember, the turtle once defeated the rabbit during a long-distance race. Staying consistent and focused will help you in your ongoing efforts to stay clean and sober. Some of your peers might appear to be doing better than you in life. That's ok; it's what makes us different from one another.

God's blessing for you might not come overnight but they are on the way. I'm sharing from experience. Do not compromise your peace of mind for instant results. Recovery is a real process. Make it happen in your life.

Take some time to discover the real you. In the words of Teddy Pendergrass, "You can't hide from yourself. Everywhere you go,

Message to People Suffering from Drug Addiction

there you are, no matter what you do." Discovering who you are and the type of person you'd like to become is the key to staying strong and consistent. Like a thief, your past addiction will be lurking right around the corner waiting for you to slip up, trying to persuade you to pick up where you left off, which is nowhere.

"If you ever fall down in life, then it is your duty to get back up because if you stay down too long, you might not have the energy to get back up."

Tio Hardiman

Acknowledgements

I would like to personally acknowledge Chinta Strausberg for inspiring me to write this book. Chinta is a remarkable woman and author who went the extra mile to secure the foreword written by Father Michael Pflieger. She also conducted several interviews for the book during the early stages of writing. Although I did not include the interviews in this version of the book, I want to pay tribute to Chinta Stausberg for her dedication and stellar work ethic, salute. Additionally, I would like to acknowledge those who helped shape my career after my addiction ended: Professor Benneth Lee, Marnell Brown, Howard Saffold, Professor Robert Starks, Professor Troy Harden, Professor John Levi, Professor Henry English, Professor Lance Williams, Professor Andy Thompson, Professor Peter St. Jean, and countless others. I would also like to thank many who are gone but not forgotten: Bobby Gore, NFL Legend Jim Brown, Karate Legend Jim Kelly, Huey P. Newton, Fred Hampton Sr, and Freedom Fighters worldwide who have lost their lives in the fight for freedom and justice. I am forever grateful for the thousands of addicts before my time that sacrificed their lives so we could have a chance at recovery.

About the Author

Tio Hardiman, Executive Director of Violence Interrupters, NFP, has dedicated his life and career to community organizing for peace and social change. Growing up in Chicago's notorious Henry Horner Housing Projects, Mr. Hardiman witnessed firsthand the devastating effects of violence and from that early exposure committed himself to ending violence in Chicago. In 1999, Mr. Hardiman joined CeaseFire, an award-winning public health model that has been scientifically proven to reduce shootings and killings. Before joining CeaseFire, Mr. Hardiman organized more than 100 block clubs to strategize community plans for public safety on behalf of the Chicago Alliance for Neighborhood Safety and held leadership positions for Bethel New Life and Chicago's CAPS Program. In 2004, Tio created the Violence Interrupters initiative.

Tio Hardiman serves as an Adjunct Professor at North Park University in the Field of Criminal Justice and Restorative Justice. Tio also worked for the Humane Society of the United States to help bring more awareness to the plight of inner-city Pitbull dog fighting which led to the End Dog Fighting Program sponsored by the U.S. Humane Society.

Mr. Hardiman is a frequent media contributor on the issues of Chicago violence and gang conflict. He has appeared on the local affiliate of every major television network, as well as CNN and the BBC. Mr. Hardiman has also been interviewed for numerous national public radio stories and has been covered by the New York Times Magazine, The Chicago Tribune, The Chicago Red Eye, Jet Magazine, The Chicago Sun Times, and numerous others. He holds a bachelor's degree in liberal arts and a master's degree in inner-city studies from Northeastern University.

References

Addiction Center. Retrieved from http://addictioncenter.com

American Addiction Centers. September 3, 2024. 12-Step Programs: 12 Steps to Recovery from Addiction. Retrieved from
https://americanaddictioncenters.org/rehab-guide/12-step

Harvard University: Center on the Developing Child. A Guide to Neglect. Retrieved from
https://developingchild.harvard.edu/science/deep-dives/neglect/

History.com Editors. May 31, 2017. Cocaine. Retrieved from
https://www.history.com/topics/crime/history-of-cocaine

Popenoe, David. January 1996. Life without Father: Compelling New Evidence That Fatherhood and Marriage Are Indispensable for the Good of Children and Society. Retrieved from
https://www.goodreads.com/book/show/472873.Life_Without_Father

Rudy, T., Perkins, D., & Wolbert, E. June 24, 2024. Desensitization to Violence: A Parent's Role. Retrieved from
https://extension.psu.edu/desensitization-to-violence-a-parents-role

Santos-Longhurst, Adrienne. February 21, 2020. Everything You Need to Know About Freebasing. Retrieved from
https://www.healthline.com/health/freebasing#freebase-vs-crack

Sills, Davia. May 26, 2023. Fatherless Daughters: The Impact of Absence. Psychology Today. Retrieved from
https://www.psychologytoday.com/us/blog/transcending-the-past/202305/fatherless-daughters-the-impact-of-absence

Wilcox, B., Wang, W., & Elhage, A. July 17, 2022. 'Life Without Father': Less College, Less Work, and More Prison for Young Men Growing Up Without Their Biological Father. Institute for Family Studies. Retrieved from
https://ifstudies.org/blog/life-without-father-less-college-less-work-and-more-prison-for-young-men-growing-up-without-their-biological-father#:~:text=Specifically%2C%20approximately%2062.5%25%20of%20boys,home%20without%20their%20biological%20father

www.ingramcontent.com/pod-product-compliance
Lightning Source LLC
Chambersburg PA
CBHW050640160426
43194CB00010B/1750